The DivaGirl's Guide to Style and Self-Respect

By Cheryl Ann Wadlington
with Sonya Beard

It's your pocketbook to success!

The DivaGirl's Guide to Style and Self-Respect

Copyright © 2012 by Cheryl Ann Wadlington

Published by
The Elevator Group, Paoli, Pennsylvania

Library of Congress Control Number: 2011922105

Trade paperback ISBN 13: 978-0-9824945-7-8

Jacket and interior design by Stephanie Vance-Patience

Published in the United States by The Elevator Group.

This is a work of non-fiction.

This book was printed in the United States.

Permissions: Quotes at the beginning of Chapters 1, 7, and 11 are used with permission of www.CloverQuotes.com. Every effort was made to determine whether previously published material included in this book required permission to reprint. If there has been an error, we apologize, and a correction will be made in subsequent editions.

To order additional copies of this book, contact:

The Elevator Group
P.O. Box 207
Paoli, PA 19301
610-296-4966 (p)
610-644-4436 (f)
www.TheElevatorGroup.com
info@TheElevatorGroup.com

Manufactured by:
Color House Graphics, Inc., Grand Rapids MI USA
March 2012

Job #36750

DivaGirl's Guide Advisory

As headmistress of an urban charm school, I've spent the past several years talking—and listening—to teen girls. The participants in my program boast a 100% graduation rate and 0% pregnancy. I'm vested in transforming today's girls into tomorrow's gems. Sometimes that means communicating in their language, on their level. Throughout the book, you will notice a conversational slang like I use in my program.

This guide will address sensitive topics like sex in the relationship chapter, "Cupid Shuffle," in an expert-approved glossary of Sexual Terms. This topic can sometimes make for awkward conversation between parents and their daughters; many times that conversation happens too late, or not at all. That is one of many essential conversations we will have here on this road map for the journey through the rocky teen years.

We changed the *names of our teen inquirers to protect their privacy.

I wanted to write a book that urban teens would pick up, read for a few pages and keep reading until the end. I've think I've done that!

Just Like You

Working in fashion is all that. It's all that you'd imagine it would be ... and a whole lot more. There's the good, the bad, and the ugly. Then there's the pretty, the fake, and the truth.

I feel like I've seen just about everything. Some things made me cringe. Some things made me cry. And then there were things that made me fall out on the floor laughing.

Being a model and modeling coach gave me a front-row seat in this industry. I've been a fashion journalist, too. So I've taken many notes throughout the years. Now I consult clients on getting their lives together, keeping it fabulous, and being the best they can be.

I've had a blast! I've rubbed shoulders with tons of celebrities. I've worked side-by-side with some of the biggest names in fashion. And I've helped ordinary people become extraordinary.

But I didn't just wake up fascinating. My life could've gone in a totally different direction. I took so many wrong turns, it's amazing I didn't end up in a ditch somewhere. But this is what I learned: It's OK to fall. Just get back up and keep on strutting. That's a DivaGirl mantra to live by!

FASHION GENES

I was hanging out in New York City with models twice my age. They were supposed to be keeping an eye on me. Their idea of babysitting was taking me to the Cheetah Club. I was only 12. Don't ask me what they were thinking.

You know those girls who look older than they are? Well, that was me. But nobody likes being scrawny and tall at that stage in life. I was really awkward. But my mother saw something special in me. She found a way to flip a negative into a positive. So she booked my schedule with fashion shows, beauty pageants, and dance classes. Now it's all a distant memory of glitter and gold.

But back then my heart was someplace else. Do you ever feel like there are a million other things you'd rather be doing? On the inside, I was more tomboy than glamour girl. I was that girl tackling the guys on the football field. But I was also that girl catwalking the runway.

I was used to the finer things in life. And, at the same time, I was rough around the edges. I walked a thin line between being a princess and a thug. My neighbors knew me as the sweetie pie next door. But my classmates knew me as the school bully. What's strange is that I never had a problem with my temper. And I never needed an excuse to throw down. Ain't that a shame?

I wish I could blame the bad influences around me, but I can't. I was my own gang leader, a lone soldier fighting way my through life. I'd been suspended from school about 10 times.

My mother was probably like many mothers: You know how they threaten to send you to a group home when you're out of control. The difference was that my mother actually did it. I forgave her ages ago, but it did take a moment for me to get over it. Now I realize it was just the reality check I needed to start acting like I had some sense.

Secret Weapon

About seven years ago, I hit the streets of Philadelphia looking for troubled girls. I knew them. I had been one of them. I wanted to show them how different their lives could be.

This was my motivation for launching the Evoluer House (www.evoluerhouse.org). It's a nonprofit agency that empowers today's young girls to think bigger, dream higher and push up the sky. We also encourage them to love the skin they're in.

The majority of girls in America feel they do not measure up in some way. And girls with low self-esteem tend to engage in harmful behavior. This can have a lasting effect on their lives. I wanted to prevent girls from heading down wrong-way streets. So I needed to start with how girls viewed themselves.

DID YOU KNOW?

- Urban teens are twice as likely to be overweight as their suburban peers.

- Urban teens are more likely to start unhealthy eating habits before they hit puberty.

- Urban teens are likely to struggle with their body image by the time they reach age 17.

The DivaGirl's Guide to Style and Self-Respect is your survival manual to navigate through the teen years. In addition to the latest techno-gadgets, every WonderGirl could use this as her trusty secret weapon. You'll learn how to survive a bad-hair day. And you'll learn how to succeed in the fashion game. And we can talk about some good decisions you can make now that will influence the rest of your life.

So SuperGirl, let's get down to it. Goodness knows you don't want to make the same mistakes I made. Time to listen up, little Divas-in-Training! I want you to learn from my story.

MY DRAMA

The youngest of six children, I'd lived a charmed life growing up in West Philadelphia. My father was a hard-working mailman, who was well respected in the community. My mother was a part-time government worker and an evangelist in the church. You've seen those prim and proper girls? Well, that was me. I was labeled a gifted child in elementary school—every teacher's dream. I was a typical daddy's girl.

But when I was in the sixth grade, my charmed life had turned chaotic. That's when my father died of a brain tumor. I didn't know how to cope. This would take a toll on my life I was too young to understand.

Counseling wasn't something we discussed then. In our community, the right herb was supposed to cure anything. And the church was supposed to have all the answers. Having emotional problems was something you kept on the hush. But there was a hole that needed to be filled. So I continued to pursue my dream of being a world-renowned dancer ... but I also started fighting.

I was a raging maniac trolling the hallways of West Philadelphia High School. No one was safe in my warpath. I slammed a boy against the locker for no good reason. I yanked off a girl's wig because I felt like it. Getting in trouble didn't scare me.

QUESTIONS:

Honestly, am I the only girl who acted a fool in high school? What's the worst thing you've done? I'm telling my story. You want to tell yours to get it off your chest? Write it down here (if it's not too horrible to print):

_____

_____

_____

_____

_____

Soon, I'd turned my rage toward a teacher. I threw a basketball at her during gym class. I don't remember if she was injured. I don't even remember why I did it. But I do remember it being the last time I was suspended from school.

My dear mother had done all she could. It was tough for all of us without my dad. My mom tried to give us a stable upbringing. But she had five other children to worry about, and she needed some help. So I was off to reform school for mischievous girls. To this day, I can't believe my own mother actually abandoned me.

When we arrived at the group home, the supervisors took one look at me and thought there had been a mistake; surely, a girl like me didn't belong there. "Give her a week," my mother responded—right before she drove away. And true to form, that's how long it took for me to turn that place out.

I spent my days with girls who came up through the foster-care system. Some were the daughters of drug addicts. Others had no parents at all. But still I stood out as the rule-breaking troublemaker. I'll never forget the many nights I was sentenced to a room with no windows and no bed. My dinner was peanut butter and jelly sandwiches. (And I couldn't stand peanut butter and jelly.)

Yet even in that hellhole, my star was shining. I was voted most popular in reform school. I was the girl everyone wanted in her crew. I realized even in lockdown, you couldn't lock down someone's spirit. Surely, I didn't belong there. I begged my mother to let me come home. Finally, she did, after one of the longest years of my life.

Second Chances

When I was released from that "prison," I was ready to get directions for the right path and stay on it. I had a long road ahead of me when I returned to school. My report card was covered with 50 Ds and Fs.

The guidance counselors had no clue how to guide me. I told them I wanted to major in fashion merchandising. They were too professional to laugh in my face. So instead they were brutally honest: "Girl, you must be crazy. No college is going to accept you with those grades."

QUESTIONS:

Are your grades ridiculous?   **Yes**   **No**

Are you trying your best in school?   **Yes**   **No**

It's never too late. What can you do now to turn things around?

_____

_____

_____

_____

_____

They weren't lying. That's exactly what the admissions office told me when I applied to Bauder Fashion College in Atlanta. I didn't listen, though. I just went with Plan B.

I applied and was accepted to Community College of Philadelphia. I scored a 3.5 GPA my first semester. Good grades came easy when I put my mind to it. I stayed for two years and took my transcripts to Bauder to see if they would reconsider me. They said, "Absolutely, we look for girls with your determination." I learned a valuable lesson:

People will be willing to invest in you if you are willing to invest in yourself.

WORKING IT

I had a blast at Bauder. Next thing you know, I was off to New York at the highly competitive Fashion Institute of Technology. And you know I was rolling with all the industry insiders there.

Then I was off to the Big Top. That's right. I joined the circus. Ringling Bros. and Barnum & Bailey recruited me as a dancer and showgirl. One year later, I was sidelined with a knee injury that ended my lifelong dream of being a Broadway dancer.

I put away my ballet slippers and tap shoes. It was time for me to help other young women get their stiletto in the door. With my Life Modeling Workshop International, I was able to mold, groom and polish young women to compete in a "chew 'em up, spit 'em out" industry. I coached many "Barbie look-alikes" on landing modeling gigs and winning beauty pageants. And I worked to get the same success for models who didn't fit into that cookie-cutter category.

BEAUTY LIES

There was a turning point in my fashion career when I had to write a magazine article about a collegiate beauty pageant in 1990. I watched brainy and beautiful girls sashay across the stage. These things rarely produced any surprises ... until a southern belle from Texas took the stage.

An exquisite plus size, she wasn't the typical contestant. But you couldn't tell her that. She packed a powder-blue satin, fringe-trimmed cowboy number like nobody else. She belted a remix of John Denver's patriotic anthem, "I'm Proud to Be an American." She wore confidence like a couture gown. She had a sense of self that was figure-forming. And she won that title.

I was overcome with emotion as I watched her being crowned. Tears were flooding down my face as I wrestled with feelings of shock and awe. I realized in that moment that this had gone against everything I had been taught—and had been teaching. I let society brainwash me into thinking that you had to be a Barbie to be successful. But she embodied a beauty queen, in the truest sense. She redefined the very word beauty.

It made me reexamine my program. What was I creating? I decided to go back to the drawing board. I understood more than ever that beauty was not one size fits all. I knew life needed to be about something more. And I wanted more for women. I needed to start from a more holistic approach—beauty from the inside out.

I was concerned with the reflections these girls saw when they looked in the mirror. I knew that I had to catch them at a young age. I didn't want them buying into media lies and beauty myths. That's why I wanted to talk to you.

GIRL TALK

Keep turning the pages of *The DivaGirl's Guide to Style and Self-Respect*. Join the conversation in "Sister 'Hood." We chat about one of a girl's most valued treasures: her girlfriends. Friendships can be tricky. One minute you're fussing. The next minute you're planning your next shopping trip like nothing ever happened. Learn how to pick them, and then learn how to keep them.

Now don't tell me I was the only little girl who played in her mother's makeup. We'll give tips on giving great face. And top celebrity makeup artists will share the tricks on getting gorgeous.

We've got to talk hair. The choices are endless with perms or naturals. We'll get to the long and short of it. There's no right or wrong way to rock your crown and glory as long as it's healthy. There's just one rule when it comes to your 'do: Work it!

Speaking of work, a DivaGirl knows that money talks. A job can be a teen's greatest investment. We'll introduce you to some young entrepreneurs who put their talent to work for them.

And we can't forget the fellas. It's no secret that teens are sexually active. No one is trying to be your mama or your minister. But you still should know that protecting your heart is important, but so is protecting yourself.

So let's get going. We can write the rules of urban etiquette together along the way. I'm just here to offer some directions. I've left plenty of free space for your input. This is your life. It's up to you! Fill in the blanks.

With Xoxo,

Ms. Cheryl

Who is a DivaGirl?

A DIVAGIRL	AN ORDINARY GIRL
Gets what she wants	Accepts what other people give her
Works a room	Hangs on the wall
Makes a strong impression	Is forgettable
Expects the best	Accepts whatever
Knows who she is	Willing to be whomever other people want
Values her reputation	Underestimates her reputation
Leads	Follows
Cherishes her image	Plays with her image
Attracts movers-and-shakers	Attracts the moved-and-shaken
Does extraordinary things	Does ordinary things
Rocks an outfit	Is rocked by her outfit
Is admired	Is tolerated
Cultivates real friends	Settles for anybody being her friend

CHAPTER 1

Who Do You Think You Are?

"The word diva to me means doing something supernatural with something natural."

—Patti LuPone
Broadway Legend

Have you ever walked in a room and it seemed like everyone was staring at you? That happened to me once. I wanted to snatch this one girl and ask, "You got a problem or something?"

I looked to see if my zipper was down. I made sure my blouse was buttoned. And I checked my view from behind to see if there were any surprises. Then the girl approached me and said, "Wow, you're really working your buzz cut. I might have to consider chopping it all off."

Was I relieved. HoneyGirl, I was grinning and twirling my fingers through my spiky locks. I thanked her and shimmied off on my merry way.

Sometimes it's like that. We don't know where a conversation is headed. Girls will look us up and down like they're wondering, "Who does she think she is?" They might say it with an attitude. Maybe it's kinda in your face. Maybe it's downright catty. Or maybe, just maybe, they're clocking our style.

Truth is, we may never know what's going through somebody's mind when they're giving us the once over. But they still pose a valid question: Who do you think you are?

When it's all said and done, it doesn't matter what they're thinking. What matters is whether we can answer that question for ourselves.

ARE YOU ...

❑ The social butterfly who loves all the attention?

❑ The quiet type who shies away from the crowd?

❑ The round-the-way girl with a serious attitude?

❑ The high-society princess who always gets her way?

❑ The fight-the-power militant who takes up the latest cause?

❑ The down-to-earth bohemian without a care in the world?

❑ The bookworm who uses her IQ as a magic wand?

❑ The talented teen with aspirations of becoming a superstar?

❑ The church-going goody two-shoes who walks a righteous path?

❑ The hardcore gangstress who runs the streets?

You know what? Don't even bother checking a box. You are much more than a label anyway. We're constantly being fed media images telling us who we should be and reminding us how we fall short. Society has a hard time defining us as individuals. So it's easier to just group us into stereotypes. But you're nobody's stereotype. Step out of the box and fill in your own description here:

_____

_____

_____

WHY?

Look, there's nobody else like you. You've got your own look, your own talents, your own gifts and your own kind of intelligence. No one else has lived your life or had your experiences. But most of all, you have your own purpose in the world. Once you get here, it's about figuring out why you're here and what you're supposed to do. It takes time. But, if you're reading this, you've already figured out that the time is now.

No one can beat you at being you if they tried. So just strive to be your best. Trying to cover somebody else's act means you're always playing second fiddle. You can't be better at being Michelle than Michelle is. If you're Kendra, you've got to be Kendra. Be you. You're unique. You have your own gift to share with the world.

And that's what this book is all about, really. We want to get to know the real you and improve on that until your star really shines. Hey, we've all got something special in us. It's just a matter of polishing it up so it sparkles.

CHECK YOURSELF

We hardly ever take a moment, look in the mirror and ask, "Who am I?" We sometimes see our-selves through the eyes of other people. We listen to what our family, teachers, and friends say about us. But the person whose opinion really counts is the one staring at you in the mirror. Do you know that girl?

So … seriously: Who are you?

Write down the top 5 things you're most talented at doing. Maybe it's sports or cooking or cheer-leading or designing funky T-shirts. Maybe it's baby-sitting. Maybe it's keeping others in check. Having trouble thinking of 5? Here are some hints:

- What do you feel good doing?
- What do people always ask you to do?
- What comes easy for you?
- What absolutely excites you?

Don't stop at 5 if you've got more. (Maybe you're just that fabulous.) Keep writing until you can't think of anything else.

Next, write down 5 good things that other people—family, friends, teachers and classmates—say about you. Same rules apply as above.

_____

_____

_____

_____

_____

Did anything not-so-good come to mind? After you get all the positive stuff down, jot down the negative stuff too, and set it aside. (We'll get back to that later.)

Now take a look at that list. How many of these things can you honestly say that you're great at doing? Which are the areas where you have the most talent or the most potential? Where do you have an edge? What makes you simply stand out from everyone else?

All that stuff, good and bad—that's you. And two things are going to happen. One: You're going to carry that with you everywhere you go. And two: Use those things to do the things you want to do in life. So your best bet is to get really up close and personal with yourself. And make it work for you.

FLIP IT

Really think about it: What is the thing that drives you crazy about yourself—the thing that you would change if you could? Write it down here.

_____

_____

_____

_____

Now ... flip it. Try seeing how the negative things you don't like about yourself or your life could be turned into something positive. For example, if you hate your skinny legs, think of them as model legs. That's what I did when folks called me "licorice legs." If your butt bothers you, think of yourself as curvy and bootylicious. Bad temper? Think of yourself as passionate. You don't have to be perfect, you just have to be yourself.

So, what's your "flip side?"

_____

_____

_____

_____

Now, every time you find yourself thinking, "I can't stand my ... " stop yourself and think of your flip side, instead. Make a list of a few ways you can use your flip side for something positive. Write that down and post it in your locker, over your mirror or somewhere that you'll see it everyday.

WHY AM I ...?

It starts at home. Maybe no one in your family finished high school, or maybe everyone has a Ph.D. Maybe your mother isn't around or maybe she hovers too much. Maybe your dad is a workaholic; maybe he's an alcoholic. Maybe you grew up in the 'hood or maybe you've moved around all your life.

Your background matters ... and it doesn't. You can look beyond where and who you are now to see the person you can be. Whether you're surrounded by doctors or drug dealers, that doesn't mean you have to follow in their footsteps. You've got to make your own path.

It's not just what's going on in your home or your neighborhood. The stuff you see on TV, the games you play, things your friends are doing—they all have an influence. It's hard to avoid. You've just got to be aware of them and how they're impacting your behavior.

Once you start paying attention, the next step is to get away from influences that are tearing you down or holding you back. When you hear something enough … eventually you'll start believing that stuff—whether it's good or bad.

LOOKING UP

Name one thing you think you might like to do in life? It can be anything. Be a singer, join the circus, go into politics, go into space … anything. What's your thing? Got it? Write it down here:

_____

_____

_____

_____

Now take a look at someone who has already succeeded at it. You may have to get on a computer and Internet search her, but I'll bet you'll find someone. No matter what you picked, there's someone who has done it or something like it. And it's likely that there's someone who is similar to you who has done it. That person can be your role model.

Having a role model helps you keep your focus on where you want to go and what you want to do. She (or he) has blazed a path to the goal you're interested in, so her (or his) life is like a map that you can follow.

This doesn't have to be someone famous. It can be your stylish aunt, a successful neighbor, an inspiring classmate. It just has to be someone you can say, "Yeah, she's doing her thing." And it's someone who makes you say, "I can do that, too!"

Sometimes you might have different role models for different things. Maybe your older sister is your family role model because she went to college. She's majoring in accounting, and you never, ever want to be an accountant, but the fact that she's doing her thing is what inspires you.

You may not know your role model personally. But you can take some cues from how she presents herself. See what kinds of things she's involved in and learn about her family life and background. Now, you do have to look at the big picture. You want to be an actress? There are hundreds you can choose from. You want to pick someone who has a similar background to you, or who looks like you, or who is living a lifestyle like you want. If she's always in court for a DUI, maybe that's not the influence you want.

Another thing about role models is that you can have as many as you want. Maybe one person is your education role model, another is your family role model, and another is your career model. When it comes to positive influences, you can't have too many.

So choose a role model. And don't sell yourself short; pick someone great. Or think of several people who are really doing it.

- Who is your role model?

_____

_____

- What do you admire about her? Why?

_____

_____

- How did she accomplish the thing you admire?

_____

_____

- What were the problems or challenges she had to overcome? How did she do it?

_____

_____

- Do you have similar challenges? How can you overcome them?

_____

_____

- What can you do to follow in her path?

_____

_____

THE REAL YOU, THE BEST YOU

It's all good. Knowing yourself, having role models, understanding who is influencing you … knowing these things alone won't get you where you want to go. You've got to take that information—and like that Mary J. Blige song goes "… Work your thing out!"

That means you not only have to stay focused, but you've got to fine-tune your skills. So break out the polish. That means you've got to know how to communicate in words and on paper. You've got to know how to talk with and get along with people. And you've got to know how to get just the right look for the situation you're in.

You've got to act like you know—no matter where you go. But don't worry, because by the time you get to the last page of this book, SuperGirl, you're going to know all that. In fact, you're going to be all that.

JUST LIKE YOU

* Neicy, 15

Q: "Who or what has had the biggest influence on the way you feel about yourself?"

Monica
Grammy Award-Winning Singer and Actress

A: "I truly believe that my family, especially my mom, has had the greatest influence on how I feel about myself both inside and out. I was always taught and told as a young person:

- To trust God in all you do
- That beauty started within
- That we are all equal
- That good treatment toward others was mandatory

All these things allowed me to live the type of life that's allowed me to be continuously blessed."

* Carson, 16

Q: "When did you recognize what made you special?"

Eve

Grammy Award-Winning Rapper and Actress

A: "This is kind of a hard question to answer. Only because there are moments in my life where I am reminded that I am special. When I use the word special, I am not implying that I am any more special than anyone else ... I'm just the exact amount of special that God made me. Since I was small, though, I've always felt I wanted to do something 'big' with my life, and I knew I didn't want to have a 'regular' life. With that being said, know that we are all gifted in some way and we are all special no matter where you come from, or who you are!

My mom has always had my back. I call her my rock all the time. She's always been my biggest supporter when it came to my music and career. That has definitely helped me get through the business.

After graduating from high school, I discussed with her my future plans [in the music industry] or going on to higher education. This was the point at which my mom encouraged me to continue pursuing my dream with music. She knew that I was only considering going to school

because I thought that this was what she would want. My mom suggested that I pursue a career in music, so that I can at least be satisfied that I made an attempt to forge a career in this direction, and have no regrets. All my mom really wanted for me was to be happy with whatever I decided I wanted to pursue. Having someone in your corner is an amazing feeling!"

Monica also weighs in on Carson's question:

A: "When I was 16, I started to realize that we are all different by design and that we are ALL special because of our differences. But I truly understood that my ability to communicate with others was special when I gave birth. Through song, love and gentle touches, I communicated with my sons before they could even speak. I think it's special when you don't have to be speaking for others to feel your sincerity and love."

Check It Out

What you see is not what was always there. When you watch the people on the stage accepting their Oscar, their Nobel Prize, their gold medal, you just see the gown, the glory and the glam. You don't see the hard work that got them there. You don't hear the voices that are still ringing in their ears that said: "Girl, you can't do that." Most successful people had to overcome obstacles to get to where they are. Need proof? Go to the library and check out some books about the people you admire or people who became well known for doing something you're interested in. Take a look at what they had to deal with to get where they are. Here are some good ones to read:

Serving From the Hip: 10 Rules for Living, Loving and Winning by Venus Williams and Serena Williams

Life Is Not a Fairy Tale by Fantasia Barrino

Miles to Go by Miley Cyrus

Put on Your Crown: Life-Changing Moments on the Path to Queendom by Queen Latifah

J Lo: The Secret Behind Jennifer Lopez's Climb To The Top by Sarah Gallick

Don't Let This Lipstick Fool You by WNBA player Lisa Leslie

Our Story by Mary Kate Olsen and Ashley Olsen

YOUR SPACE

It's all yours. Take the next few lines below to write down something you learned about yourself from reading this chapter. Anything here you never really thought about before? Anything that you're going to pay attention to? Anything that you want to explore more closely? Think about your role models. Who are they? What are they doing? What about their lives are worth copying? What about their lives are not worth copying? Use this space to communicate with yourself about yourself.

_____

_____

_____

_____

_____

CHAPTER 2

Style Star

"I like what I see when I'm looking at me
when I'm walking past the mirror."

—Mary J. Blige
Just Fine

It's all about the look! I'm talking about a Kodak moment. That's when you are just too cute—done up, from head to toe. Nobody can tell you a thing. My moment was when I was a young teen.

I was rocking a white faux fur mini and vest, a purple puffy-sleeve blouse, matching tights and white Go-Go boots. My curly hair was is in a foot-high ponytail pulled so severe it made my eyes squint. I put the V in vogue.

Have you ever had a style moment? When you were so cute you couldn't stand yourself? We often feel good when we do. For some of us, accessorizing can be a hobby. And clothes can be an all-out obsession.

Styling is our chance to express ourselves every time we step out the house. Our creativity can take us anywhere we want to go—downtown boho-chic to uptown cosmo-glam.

Great style is not about the clothes you're rocking: It's how you rock the clothes. And it's not about blazing labels, either. It's about putting together a look that's uniquely you.

You're about to hear from our celebrity glam squad, assembled just for you. They'll give you the basics that every girl can use to look—and feel—fabulous. We're talking all-time, A-number-one, never-fail fashion dos.

SHE'S GOT TO HAVE FIT

The glam squad's best-ever fashion tip: Learn to love your body, flaws and all. Knowing what works and what doesn't for your body shape is your ticket to having a signature style. But a girl's got to know and own up to what shape she is. (I mean your real shape, not the Halle Berry-shape you might pretend to have.) Which shape best describes you?

Check the appropriate box below.

❏ **Slender-Shaped:** Your body is slim with small breasts and hips and/or bottom.

❏ **Top-Heavy:** Your body is curvy, smaller on bottom and heavier on top like an upside-down triangle. Your bust is the most dominant part of your body. Your hips and bottom are smaller.

❏ **Pear-Shaped:** Your upper body is smaller than your lower body. You may have narrow shoulders and a small bust. You may have wide hips or big thighs or a round bottom. The majority of women have pear shapes. And so do **Christina Aguilera**, **Alicia Keyes** and **Jennifer Lopez**.

❏ **Curvaceous:** Your body has an hour-glass shape. You may have large breasts, a small waist, and wide hips or big bottom.

Let's talk about tips for styles that work best for you. If you are …

Illustrations by Waren K. Bradley

SLENDER-SHAPED

Jeans: Low rise, straight leg and boot-cuts may be really cute on you. You can even do styles with pockets and designs if you want your rear end to look curvier.

Skirts: Material with Lycra or spandex will suit your body. Draping would be a nice touch. Knee-length skirts show off your legs best. Pencil, A-line, and long skirts work fabulously. And try some with pockets.

Dresses: Shirt dresses and shift dresses are your go-to looks. Sheaths and tunics are also stunners in your closet. You can pull off a coat dress, too. A fitted bodice, a tapered waist, and a full skirt add a little oomph. Strapless dresses are a good look, but spaghetti straps look better.

Tops: Blouses with ruching look dazzling on this body type. Crisp white button-downs are sharp. You can also go with sleeveless tanks, polos, and V- and U-necks.

Jackets: Single-breasted blazers are a winning look for you. The jacket should come down to the hip bone or longer. A V-neckline down to your cleavage will draw attention away from your waist. Tapered slacks that flare at the hips create a curvy look.

Suits: Wear confidence in a flared jacket that matches a smooth A-line skirt or boot-cut pants. You can also set it off with a jacket that hits below your hip with a shorter pencil skirt.

Illustrations by Waren K. Bradley

Top Heavy

Pants: Cigarette pants with a high waist will flatten your tummy. Look for ones with Lycra to mold your shape. Need to balance narrow hips and wide shoulders? Try a wide-leg or boot-cut trouser.

Jeans: Boot-cut or skinny jeans are just for you. Jeans with a slight flare at the bottom can give you that dreamy hourglass figure. Side pockets will get your hips more attention. And cargo-style pockets will balance out the bottom.

Skirts: For a classy silhouette, look for multilayered or flared skirts. These styles will enhance your hips. Finish the look with a belt to cinch in the waist.

Dresses: Drape-style dresses will even out your body shape and whisper elegance. To flatter a large bust, V-necks will work wonders to lengthen the neck.

Tops: Go for adorable in floaty blouses. Draping is the key for a smooth and seamless look up top. Try fabrics in a soft jersey that won't cling.

Jackets/Suits: Grab attention in a V-neck blazer in a fun color. An A-line skirt will skim your hips and accentuate your shape. To round out your bottom half, add volume with a kick-flared hem.

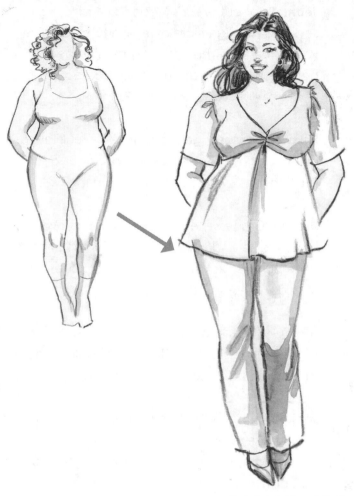

Illustrations by Waren K. Bradley

CURVACEOUS-SHAPED

Pants: Your best bet is a flat-front trouser with a low waist. The hips can be a little fitted with a fuller straight leg. Boot-cuts and subtle flares get the job done, too.

Jeans: Your fashion closet needs stretch denim in darker washes. Boot-cuts are preferred. Go for styles that are higher in the back and lower in front. Angled pockets will work better than flat pockets.

Skirts: High waistbands are darling on you. Pencil and trouser skirts will flatter your figure. Be careful not to go too short. Your skirts look best when they hit above the knee. Choose darker colors so your upper half stays balanced.

Dresses: Have a party with fitted dresses. The wrap dress is a staple for you. Semi-fitted tunics and tapered-waist sheaths are très chic. And we say yes to strapless.

Tops: Semi-fitted styles will show off your hourglass figure. So will a halter top. Strapless, off-the-shoulder, and crossover tops are fashionable options for you. And go on and rock a turtleneck. Medium-size prints are OK. Punch it up with a tuck or belted style.

Jackets/Suits: Command respect in single-breasted styles fitted at the waist. Jackets flared at the hem also do it for you. Pair your jackets with pencil skirts or straight-leg trousers. And belt the jacket.

Illustrations by Waren K. Bradley

PEAR-SHAPED

Pants: A boot-cut can be magic for slimming hips and thighs. A low-waist will minimize your lower half and balance your upper half. Flat-front trousers with

a small waistband will pull in your mid-section.
Straight or wide-legged pants are becoming on you.

Jeans: Like pants, a straight style is the way to go.
And work those boot-cuts. You'll need a low rise.
Take it easy with the pocket embellishments. It's
cool to tuck this style into knee-high boots.

Dresses/Skirts: Empire-waist styles and wrap
dresses were designed with you in mind. Opt for
embellishments on the bodice. Just hit that hem-
line at the knee. Flared and A-line skirts are sophisticated choices. Try dark bottoms with
lighter-colored tops.

Tops: Sparkle in colors, prints, bows, ruffles, wraps,
and horizontal stripes. Almost any neckline—
V-neck, U-neck, boat, ballet, square, sweetheart,
crew, mandarin—looks good on you. Tailored
tops are your thing. Make sure they're down to the
hipbone. Halters and camisoles are also beautiful
on you.

Jackets/Suits: Strut your stuff in jackets that hit at
the hipbone. Styles tapered at the waist with slight
shoulder padding are a home-run. Get an A-line
skirt or trousers to round out the look.

Fashion Popo

Come on, MissGirl. I mean there was a reason the three-way mirror was invented. Yet some of us leave the house in what we call fashion no-nos. Or should we call them fashion oh-no-she-didn'ts? As your friendly neighborhood style watch, we've been on the street patrolling the fashion scene. You may have seen outfits that we've given the green light. Now these outfits have been given the red light, as in you STOP playing, turn around, go home and change.

Stop It!

The Cleavage Queen look is perfect for XXX-rated porn stars. If you're going for a more fashion-forward look that doesn't scream streetwalker, stay away 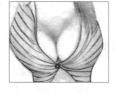 from this boob job. It could get you fired.

 Beware of **Booty Bearing** shirts disguised as dresses. You know that mess is too short. Dresses, shirts, and shorts should be long enough to cover your assets. If you can't bend over without showing your goodies, head straight to jail, do not pass go.

No one can pull off the **Muffin-Top** effect no matter how gorgeous they are. Your gut spilling out of your clothes is just not attractive. Let the mirror be your friend. And remember this: If it doesn't fit, you ought to quit.

Express your fashion sense, but don't reveal **Too Much Info**. Low-rise jeans aren't for every figure. You should be able to sit, bend and dip while leaving some things

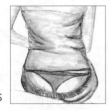

to the imagination. You don't want to get pulled over for flashing people.

GO FOR IT!

✓ Cool, colorful dresses brighten your wardrobe.

✓ Flatter your curves with the proper fit.

✓ Crisp white shirts are always a classic.

✓ The little black dress is a must-have in your closet.

✓ Perfect-fit jeans never go out of style.

✓ Chic hairdos complement every outfit.

✓ Fun footwear can give your look the lift it needs.

CURVES AHEAD

Some girls have curves. We tend to be more round than other women. So we need to pay special attention to ensure we get the proper fit. Clothes aren't always cut to fit fuller body shapes. You also might have to graduate from shopping in the junior department to the women's department, where the clothes are fuller cut. Don't worry; they have super trendy and better quality items there.

Please, please, please try before you buy. Go ahead and take those jeans back to the dressing room. Now give them a test run: Bend, squat, walk, and sit to make sure everything is still in place and comfortable before you make a purchase. Whenever you shop, try on clothes with the actual shoes and undergarments you'd be wearing. A girl's got to know if that piece is going to work for her before she leaves the store.

Celebrity stylist **Debra Ginyard** has some helpful tips. She's helped many starlets look their best, including **Alicia Keys, Heather Matarazzo, Lauryn Hill,** … and now you. Here's how to get the proper fit:

- The shoulder seam of a garment should be aligned with the tip of your shoulder bone.

- You should never have to tug a jacket, dress, or pants to make them cover your derrière.

- The garment should fall naturally over the hips, unless it's a stretch material. If it doesn't, it's too small. Leave the garment in the store.

- A skirt should never rise up in the front or back. The side seams should fall naturally, in a vertical-line formation.

- Long sleeve items should stop at base of wrist.

- On any item, the buttons should not pull.

- Bodice darts should match the pointed area of your bust line. It should not fall below them or above them.

- And whatever you do, remember just because a garment is made in your size, that doesn't mean the garment will look right on your body shape.

What Lies Beneath

Our undies are just as important as our outerwear. You might be able to get away with hot-pink underwear and avoid a total fashion disaster. But MissGirl, underwear is not to be seen. Still then, we can tell if you're wearing the right kind. Proper panties and befitting bras can make or break an outfit. So stay safe with neutral shades close to your skin tone and consider the following:

Visible Panty Lines

Countless women are guilty of committing this fashion faux pas. The dreaded VPL, which can kill a look, is avoidable. Here's how:

- Thongs are your solution to VPL. They get rid of the bottom line.

- Choose panties with smaller stitching or subtle hemlines. Seamless panties also do the trick.

- Wear snug boy shorts, boxers, or women's boxer-briefs to hide VPL.

- Avoid VPL by choosing panties with the proper fit and correct size. It's all about having a smooth, bulge-free look.

Bust Lines

Bras are one of the most key pieces in our boudoir. A well-fitting bra does two things: holds 'em and shapes 'em. It supports and it enhances. But in order to find one, first you have to know your real size. Here are some important tips for getting the right fit from **TeenHealth.org**.

Our breasts grow fast during teen years. They will continue to change, too. Your bra size may keep changing. While you're still developing, you could invest in fewer bras. Get measured often and double-check your size.

Consider hooks, wires, and other hazards. Before you buy your next bra, ask yourself this: How will this hold me up for the next 18 hours? You don't want that front closure popping out of the blue. Are the straps comfortable? Will they cause friction with your backpack?

Try this test: Lift your arms in the air and put them back down by your side. Does your bra ride across your breasts? If yes, then the band is too loose. You want support from your sports bra? Jump up and down to check for bounce control.

To get a feel for how you'd look in the real world, try on the bra with your top. Watch for embellishments on the bra. How do they look under your T-shirt or sweater? You may want to rethink the designs.

Sizes may vary, but two things are key to being bra happy: comfort and fit. Keep trying on a variety until you find the right one for you ... the same way you would for a pair of jeans.

Go see the bra-fit experts. They can change the way you look—and feel. Check at your major department stores or lingerie boutiques.

BOOBY TRAPS

It's true about 8 out of 10 women wear the wrong size bra, although they may not realize it.

Falling prey to the wrong size causes these reactions: "Oooh …

- She has booby spillage."

- Her clothes aren't draping her body properly."

- Her rolls and bulges show through her top."

- Her breasts aren't even supported."

- Her boobs are bouncing every which way."

BARE ESSENTIALS

- **Flat seam** thongs give line-free looks for pants.

- **Seamless** boy shorts work well under dresses and skirts.

- **Casual bras** made of cotton work for everyday.

- **Fancy bras** of satin blends will look smooth under dressier styles.

- **Sports bras** will provide firm support if you're involved in physical activity.

- **Slips** are sometimes necessary for your dresses. Half-slips will do for skirts. If you're wearing a sheer or see-through number, that's when a slip will come to the rescue.

RED CARPET OCCASIONS

Long, black evening gowns are like standard uniforms at tux-and-tails affairs. These days, though, formal-wear options are endless—at least for us girls. You're young and beautiful, so go ahead and be daring and different. Just keep it classy.

First, look for attire made of elegant fabrics that shimmer, sparkle, and stand out in the crowd. We're talking satins, silks, and velvets. Any material that has metallic or a nice sheen are stunners. Do some beaded embellishments, rhinestones or crystals, and you'll dazzle the crowd.

Be bold and skip the gown, if you want to put your own twist on things. Wearing a two-piece ensemble gives you the go-ahead to be creative so you can mix and match.

An ankle-length skirt with embroidery is a stylish take on formal. Or a floor-length skirt that flares like a ballerina can be ever so regal. A long slim skirt, with a velveteen texture, would be exquisite.

And if you really want to take it there, wear the pants, DivaGirl. Being able to pull off fitted slacks or wide-legged pants, in satin or velvet, says you can write your own rules when it comes to fashion.

If you do a skirt or pants, find the right top to complete your look. Think spaghetti-strap camisoles, strapless silky tops, and halters. If the event is on the conservative side, throw on a shawl with some sheen or sparkle.

By now we know black is always the new black. Still, explore other colors in rich jewel tones to add a little pizzazz. Royal blues, emerald greens, and ruby reds will sizzle in a sea of dark colors. And metallic silvers and golds turn up the volume with any ensemble.

PROM PREP

A dress that's revealing too much of what your mama gave ya? HoneyGirl, save that drama for the school play. Many schools set dress codes for proms, and you do not want to be sent home or attract the wrong kind of attention for showing up at the prom dressed half naked.

COUNTDOWN TO PROM

Review this checklist to help you prep for your big day.

THE BUDGET   TOTAL: $_____

Be realistic. How much money do you have to burn? And who will be coughing up the cash? Got a figure in your head? Now go down this list and plug in some numbers.

THE TUX

If you want to be coordinated, you may have to help your date with this one. Help him choose a color scheme that will match your look.

THE APPOINTMENTS   COST: $ _____

Will you need hair extensions or will you go for an elegant updo? Will your makeup be done by a professional? What about your mani/pedi? Book a spot (a month in advance) before all the slots are taken.

THE DRESS   COST: $ _____

Pick the perfect dress. You want to smile when you look at your prom pictures 10 years from now. So go with a classy, timeless formal dress. Does it need to be ordered (3 months in advance), purchased (2 months in advance) or altered (1 month advance)?

THE ACCESSORIES   COST: $ _____

It's time to accessorize: Will you be wearing family jewels or do you need to buy or rent jewelry? What will work with your dress and hairdo? You want to sparkle … but no need to light up like a Christmas tree.

THE PURSE   COST: $ _____

An evening bag can be a lifesaver. Leave the
backpack at home. Carry some mad money, cell
phone, lipstick, and blush and call it an evening.

THE SHOES   COST: $ _____

Break those walkers in (one month in advance).
You can be cute and comfortable. It will save you
from limping around all night.

THE BOUTONNIERE   COST: $ _____

Don't forget you need to get your date a bouton-
niere, which is a little flower that goes in his lapel.
Order this from your nearest flower shop (two
weeks in advance).

THE CORSAGE

Remind your date that he needs to order your flower.

THE DATE

School your date on how to greet your parents.
Calm his nerves. And encourage your parents to
be considerate of his feelings.

THE FRIENDS

Discuss the evening, driving concerns, alcohol,
sexual expectations, and other potentially sticky
issues with friends.

BE YOUR OWN SUPERSTAR

If you want celebrity style on your special day, celebrity fashion stylist **Debra Ginyard** has a warning: "You can't use Beyoncé as a style muse and say I want to look like her with a particular dress or style. You have to ask yourself, 'Do I have a Beyoncé body type?' She is a performer and clothes are custom made for and with her in mind."

GLOBE TROTTING

A girl can easily add some international spice to her wardrobe. The goddess look from Ancient Greece always pops up on the red carpet. It's simple with an off-the-shoulder gown or strapless asymmetrical dress. And then find some strappy Roman-style sandals, and you're ready for battle.

Map out some ways to add cultural touches to your wardrobe:

AFRICA

This where it all started—civilization and style. Watch the runways to see where designers get their inspiration when they need to combine patterns, and add a little boldness and soul to their collections. Nobody does jewelry like they do in the Motherland. Handcrafted big disc earrings, multi-layered chokers, and chunky bangles have been fashion must-haves for centuries.

ASIA
Colorful or bedazzled chopsticks are fun hair accessories. Make your own obi sash or use a cummerbund—wrap it over a shirt, and sport it with jeans. Mandarin tops add a little flair of the Far East to your wardrobe. And check out the wild style of Tokyo's Harajuku girls online for some more uniquely cool tips.

EUROPE
Outlandish and eclectic street-style rules. Work some cute little feminine dresses or flared skirts into the mix. What about kooky-cool school-girl plaids? Or break out the Bermuda shorts with an artsy hat. Tribal fashion-forward looks grace the streets of London: Pair a tribal print jacket, blouse, or sweater with jeans.

SOUTH AMERICA
Channel a vibrant flamenco dancer with a pretty flower in your hair, ruffled tiered skirt, and peasant blouse. Be sure to dream in vivid colors like red, orange, and bright blue that will bring out the flavor. Classic or trendy ponchos will give you a little spunk.

And big and chunky accessories, like a beaded necklace, will complete an edgy, yet girlie look.

COLOR PLAY

When it comes to teen girls, many rules for wearing color don't apply. Play with color. Have fun and experiment with different shades and tones and hues. The brighter, the better. Neons and fluorescents are fine in small doses. You don't want to blind people or be mistaken for a traffic sign. But you do want to stand out. Bright colors make people happy and put us in a good mood. If you wear colors well, it shows that you've got some serious confidence.

SUITING UP

School is fine for flaunting your style. When it comes to the workplace however, we've got to pull it together. Sure, job interviews are based on experience and personality. But trust that the interviewer is looking you up and down, taking notes. So appearance matters! If you're shabby, your résumé and background may not be enough. Check out these guidelines on the following page for a polished interview outfit.

DO IT, GIRL!	DON'T EVEN THINK ABOUT IT!
Choose dark solid colors for pants, skirts, and suits and you'll cream the competition.	Showing up in capri pants, leggings, jeans, sweats? Somebody call the fashion cops!
Wear skirts no more than two inches above the knee and you're on a roll.	Coming in a short skirt or mini dress? You're in big trouble!
Layer a dressy tank with a blazer or cardigan and no one can touch you.	Wearing a strapless or spaghetti-strap dress? You know better!
Don dressy button-down shirts, neatly tucked in and you're in business.	Sporting a midriff-baring top, low neckline or see-through fabric? Stop it!
Have neatly trimmed nails with clear or neutral colors and you're good to go.	Having long fang nails, chipped polish or wild colors? What are you thinking?
Rock just one ring per hand and one bracelet or watch and that's all you need.	Showing up with visible body piercing and tattoos? Seriously? Do you want this job?
Be on time, be confident and be enthusiastic.	Chewing gum or smoking cigarettes are so not cute.

*Are you kinda iffy on what to wear? If so, grab a girlfriend, neighbor or an aunt. Let them be the judge.

MY STYLE LIST

Yeah, you're still working out your style and keeping up with the trends. By the time high school rolls around, there are some basics every DivaGirl should have in her closet. Here's a list of how to start building a functional wardrobe that will last for years:

JEANS

- Find a pair of super sick jeans that look like they were made just for you. Don't break the bank though.

- Stick to a darker denim that can go from day to evening.

- Try a classic straight-leg or slight flare (boot-cut). Trendy styles come and go, so skip the skinny jeans or extra-wide legs.

PANTS

- Great black pants are always a keeper. Simple-chic styles rule. Who needs all those embellishments? It limits your ability to mix and match.

- Khakis are a staple. Or you can rock a pair of slacks in tan or beige.

SHIRTS

- Every girl should have a crisp white shirt.

- A plain black shirt will come through for you again and again.

- A rainbow selection of tanks will round out your wardrobe.

CARDIGANS/SWEATERS
- Try a burst of bold primary colors here. You can crank out some patterns and prints, too. Jeans and basic color pants can be paired with anything. So have fun with leopard, paisley, floral, or sequin.

JACKETS/COATS
- If it's freezing, go for a heavy coat in a rich color. What about berry? For milder weather, do a lightweight coat in a fun color.

- A classic denim jacket will go with almost any everyday outfit.

- Leather jackets can really amp up your outfit.

DRESSES/SKIRTS
- A denim skirt would be fun if it comes mid-thigh and fits properly.

- A plain black skirt two inches above the knee is always in order.

- A fancy little black dress can be your go-to number for special occasions.

- Three casual dresses and skirts: Dress them up or dress them down, according to your mood.

SHOES

- Flats are here to stay, so get jazzy with different colors and styles.

- Dressy shoes are the way to go when you're at church or out on the town.

- Tennis shoes can be dope, even classic in some cases, in girlie colors.

INSIDER TIPS

- Try sporty separates to mix and match with other things in your closet.

- Buy what you love, not what others like for you.

- Great style is a learned art, and you're the artist-in-training.

- Select vibrant colors in touchable fabrics to put you in a happy mood.

SPEND-A-RELLA STORIES

Show us a female who doesn't love a bargain, and we'll get her some professional help. You want a real steal? Let's go shopping at the end-of-the-season sales. That's when we find all kinds of slamming outfits for a giant fraction of the price.

Mark your calendars, HoneyGirl. The best time to shop and save is January and February for fall fashions. Want to get some fantastic spring pieces, shop mid-June, July, and August.

Bargain Hunting

Department stores are packed. And the teen chain stores can be crazy crowded, too. You look around, you've spent too much, and everybody is looking the same. Sometimes, we've got to mix it up a little. Try visiting these places to spice up your closet and save some pretty pennies while you're at it:

- **Swap Parties** You host/attend a party at, say, a coffee shop or a public park. Bring something fly you can't fit or don't mind sparing. Invite about 10 other girls to do the same. One girl's hand-me-down is another girl's hook-me-up.

- **Consignment Shops** Hunt for vintage-looking pieces to add to your modern look. You may even stumble across some designer trends. You never know, so it's always worth the visit.

- **Sample Sales** are legendary for getting those sky-high priced designer pieces for less. The sizes run ridiculously small, but you've got to dig. Sometimes you can find banging accessories if nothing else. Check online for locations.

- **Military Outlets** have sporty looks that may give your wardrobe an edge. Be a soldier and take a browse through your local Army-Navy stores and see what matches your style.

- **Boys Department** If you're petite you can save in this department on basics and save a bundle while you're at it. Sometimes guys get all the breaks.

- **Boutiques** These high-end shops will keep you standing out in the crowd with some original looks and designer price tags. If you've got it like that, go for it.

*Check online for store coupons. No joking. You may snag up to 10 percent or 25 percent off. Be a coupon queen!

SHOPPING TIPS

- Say pretty please to the sales staff. Ask if they'll give you a heads-up about upcoming sales. You know they know all the good deals.

- Join the mailing list at your favorite stores. You may be invited to special events or get additional discounts.

- Double-check clothes for cosmetics around the neck area. Pass up anything that is stained.

- Ask for a discount if it's damaged and you've just got to have it.

- Take full advantage of those layaway payment plans. That's why they have them.

- Keep receipts. Don't be ashamed if you need to make returns or exchanges.

MADE TO MEASURE

My Stats – Write them down and update (have your measurements taken) every six months. You never know when you'll stumble upon a hot fashion find with your name written all over it. You want to be ready to snag it.

- Height _____
- Weight _____
- Bust & cup size _____
- Waist _____
- Hips _____
- Tee Shirt _____
- Shirt _____
- Dress _____
- Skirt _____
- Pant _____
- Jacket _____
- Shoe _____
- Inseam _____

Just Like You

* Nicole, 15

Q: "I don't have much to spend on clothes. How can I be stylish on a budget?"

Rakia Reynolds
The Fashion Ambassador, Philly360.com

A: "A fashionista doesn't plan her wardrobe according to her budget; a real fashionista dresses according to how an outfit makes her feel. My budget allows me to purchase pieces that are transformable so I can wear them repeatedly without being obvious.

Every young woman needs these three things in her closet:

- A basic black blazer. It's a staple piece that will never go out of style and it can be paired with jeans, a pencil skirt, and a jumper with heels to dress it up (my favorite).

- Coats, cardigans, and blazers are an integral counterpart to everyday wear. When you have great outerwear, you can never go wrong.

- A little black dress—as cliché as it may sound— will take you a long way.

- A pair of pumps/heels—not stilettos; you can save those for the party. Sometimes putting on a fun

pair of pumps (in any color that makes you feel special) puts you in a better mood. You'll walk differently, stand taller, and feel more confident.

- Vintage! Vintage! Vintage! Become familiar with the vintage and thrift stores in your neighborhood. Big designers that we all know and love are constantly on the hunt for items in these stores that they can replicate. You can be the trendsetter and have the original!

- I have my go-to places to find steals when I can't splurge (this is quite often). At Loehmann's, you can find amazing deals up to 75 percent off in their Back Room section. Greene Street Consignment Shops, found nationwide, are the epitome of a great find. And check out Marshall's.

- My college professors would always tell me to dress up when taking tests. At first it was a pain in the neck, because I wanted to roll out of my bed with sweats and sneakers like everyone else. But as a business student, I was required to take things seriously, especially test-taking and presentation. In the long run it taught me a lot, and since I look at life as an everyday test, my heel-wearing days are still here!"

* Gloria, 17

Q: "I want guys to notice what's on the inside without having to reveal too much too soon of what's on the outside. Is this realistic?"

Celebrity Fashion Stylist Micah Lamar
(Clients include: Lindsay Lohan, Jennifer Hudson, Leah Renee)

A: "Yes! This is realistic, and it is good that that's where your mind is. The way to go about doing this is in how you present yourself from the start. As a stylist, I know how to portray a certain look just by dressing a certain way. Always present yourself like a lady, and you'll be treated like one. Also, attract guys with your brain and your personality. Show guys that you are cool, funny, and smart! That's what will get you the respect and attract the right guys you deserve."

CHAPTER 3

Sister 'Hood

"Sometimes you have to choose and then
you'll see if your friend is true [she'll] be there
with you through the thick and thin."

—TLC, R&B Super Trio
What About Your Friends

Now tell the truth. Did you have an imaginary
friend when you were a little girl? I mean who
didn't? She was probably perfect, too. And for
whatever reason, you liked her better than everybody else.

You could tell her any and everything. You never
had to worry about her spreading your business in
the street. And she always did the things you
enjoyed doing.

At an early age, we girls realize how crazy-cool friendships can be. Back then, we just needed a gal pal to hang around, who could play dress up, and share our invisible tea.

Friendship is always a juicy topic. Girl groups were singing about it way before Diana Ross & The Supremes. And they'll continue singing about it long after Destiny's Child. It's one of the most meaningful bonds a girl will have in her lifetime.

LADIES FIRST

Nothing compares to having a good, good, good girlfriend … our ace boon coon. During the teen years, friends become even more important as life gets a little tougher than playing house. She's the one who'll be there to give you high-fives when you're doing your thing. She'll challenge you when you've stepped out of line. She'll have your back when you need an extra hand. And she'll pick up the pieces when things fall apart. Rarely will one girl be all those things all the time, so you may need a few friends to round out your crew.

There are 1,001 rules of friendship under the sun. We're not even going to begin to talk about them here. However, one tip applies far beyond the laws of friendship. It's so valuable, it's a golden rule: "Treat your friends the way you want to be treated." It's just that simple. And you've probably heard it your whole life. But think about what it means. If you put it into practice, you'll probably become a better friend to other people. And you'll probably attract better friends to you.

You're at an age when you might go through best friends as often as you change shoes. But real friendship is a treasure that doesn't come along every day. And like most treasures, only time will reveal their true sense of value. This is probably something to consider when you're making new friendships and maintaining old ones. It's fine to second-guess friendships along the way, but think twice before you decide to dump her.

CHOOSING FRIENDS

I remember the girls who only wanted to hang with the cool clique or the girls they thought were pretty. But the reality is good friends come in all designs, shapes and sizes, colors and creeds.

So how do you decide which girls to run with and which girls to run from? Maybe speak to that girl who resembles someone you already know. If she's around your age, if she lives in your neighborhood, if she's new at school, give her a shout out. See where it goes. You don't have to make any commitments.

Remember, sometimes we just like to window shop for new friends. So we don't have to make any purchases until we're ready.

If you're the shy type, try this sisterly advice:

- Everybody appreciates a good listener. So try not to hog the conversation. If she dozes off during your stories, that's probably not a good sign.

- And be reciprocal: If your friend is doing and giving of herself with you, do the same for her.

- And while you're busy making new friends, don't forget about the coolest friend any girl could ever have: herself. If you enjoy your own company, you'll never be lonely.

HIM OR HER?

"Boyfriends come and go," but you know how that saying ends: "Girlfriends are forever." OK, that may not always be the case. But if we had to bet money, a good girlfriend usually sticks around a lot longer than the guy.

Don't get it wrong, guys are great, too. They can offer a male point of view. But your girls are there for you in ways guys are not. Some things guys just don't get. And we know most guys couldn't walk in our pumps if they tried.

Chances are your girlfriends have gone through or will go through similar situations as you have. If they haven't, they know someone who has. Here's a good question: Who do you run to when a guy has shown you his true colors?

Are your girls forgiving when you come running to them after they took a backseat to your latest love interest? That's called loyalty. Remember this before you decide to drop everything for him when he comes calling.

Believe me, absence does make the heart grow fonder. Look at it this way: If you give him all your time, he may not value the time you spend with him. There's nothing wrong with letting a guy know you do have a life aside from him. Even if you don't, it may be a good idea to act like you do. It's never a bad move to spend some quality time with your girls.

NV

Some of us hear this all the time. A girl will say, "She's just envious of me." Envy is this green monster that tends to make some people want what others have. It can be superficial things (clothes or car), physical beauty (long hair or long legs) or talented gifts (beautiful voice or brilliant mind).

But HoneyGirl, the green monster has bad vision. It only lets you see the good things someone has. You never notice the bad. So that girl who looks like she has it all together? You really may not know what her true story is. If you did know her back-story, you may be glad you didn't trade places with her. Everyone's life is a package deal; it includes the good with the bad.

If you ask the old folks, they'll say, "SweetiePie, envy is nothing but counting someone else's blessings instead of your own." You always have a reason to be thankful. So the next time that green monster starts to creep up, just chill.

Everything will be straight if you turn those negative thoughts into something positive. You should've seen one of the DivaGirls in my program. She was constantly checking how much her friends had. Then she started volunteering at a soup kitchen, working with families in need. And she realized just how good she had it. And you know what? She sent that green monster limping back to his cave.

Envy doesn't always have to be a green monster. Sometimes it can be a great motivator. Just flip it. Say to yourself, "If she can reach that goal, I know I can, too." Use it as a way to define your own standards for success.

Take some notes. We don't need to hate on someone else's achievements. What they've shown you is proof that dreams are possible. If someone has dramatic weight loss, that's proof that pounds do come off (with hard work). If someone lands a plum job, that's proof that some companies will take a chance on young people.

Are you one of those girls on the ball? Perhaps there's somebody who's envious of you. Who could blame them? Now how do you handle it? Write your response below:

_____

_____

_____

_____

_____

OR YOU COULD TRY THIS APPROACH:

Encourage your friend and tell her that she has potential, too. She may need a little boost. Saying something like this may do the trick: "Hey I did this, I bet you could achieve what you wanted to do. Let me know if I can help."

Give her the low-down. Was it a lot of hard work to get where you are? Sharing your personal story may inspire her.

At the end of the day, you have to live your own life. There will always be haters. And you can't please everybody. So don't worry or break a nail trying.

Just Like You

* Brittany, 14

Q: "Why do females go against other females?"

DJ Diamond Kuts
Producer, Tour DJ, and Host of BET's The Deal

A: "Some girls may be insecure or unhappy with themselves. When they see qualities in another girl that they don't have, they can become jealous and express their feelings in a negative way.

But it's OK to be able to identify with someone that has it going on. The thing is, what do you do with that information? Do you allow it to give you an excuse for you not to like that person? Or do you take that information and use it to inspire yourself? It doesn't always have to be something big like losing a whole bunch of weight. It could just be a way to inspire you to have a better attitude throughout the day."

Take It To The Street

Friendships don't usually fall into your lap. Sometimes you have to go on a little fishing trip.

- For your bait just start with a simple "hello." You'd be amazed at how powerful this word can be. You'll be surprised at how it is the start of many lasting friendships.

- Compliments always go a long way, don't they? When you debut your fierce haircut, you want people to notice. Other girls feel the same way.

- When you keep in touch, you can keep the friendship from fizzling. Follow up with a phone call or a quick e-mail, so she doesn't think you're a ghost.

The next time you're out and about, remember you could be crossing paths or sitting next to your future BFF.

FRIENDSHIP TEST

1. How well do you know your friend?

   A. I know her like the back of my hand.

   B. I'm still trying to figure her out.

   C. Sometimes I don't know her at all.

   D. Explain:

2. What's the coolest thing your friend has done for you?

_____

_____

_____

3. What's the foulest thing your friend has done to you?

_____

_____

_____

4. How does she treat you when you get around other people?

_____

_____

_____

5. How does she treat you behind your back?

_____

_____

_____

6. Does she compliment you on your success?

                                        Yes   No

7. Does she ever try to put you down?   **Yes   No**

8. Can you squash things when you have an argument?

Yes   No

9. Does she come through for you when you need her or does she leave you hanging?

_____

_____

_____

10. Why do you want/need friends anyway?

A. Companionship—so you're not lonely

B. Protection—in case other people mess with you

C. Support—to have someone share your ups and downs

* There are no right or wrong answers to these questions. They are just to help you evaluate your friendships.

YOUR SPACE

Now let's meet some of your crew. Make a list of your friends and acquaintances. Examine and evaluate the quality of your friendships.

Think about your neighbors. Who's the girl in your 'hood you can turn to because she's always ready to listen? Who's the girl in your congregation you cut up with in Sunday School because you both would rather be some place else? Maybe there's a girl you've known since first grade who keeps you on your toes. Include them, too:

_____

_____

_____

_____

Do you have any "friends" who put your business in the street or talk smack behind your back? Who are the girls in your circle who share none of your goals? Think about the girls who influence you in a negative way.

_____

_____

_____

_____

CHECK IT OUT
Meet some cool girls like you at these girl groups and programs.

Black Girls Rock! is a non-profit youth empowerment and mentoring organization established to promote the arts for young women of color ~ **www.blackgirlsrockinc.com**

Girls For A Change (GFC) is a national organization that empowers girls to create social change ~ **www.girlsforachange.org**

Girls Inc. is a nonprofit organization that inspires all girls to be strong, smart, and bold through a network of local organizations in the United States and Canada ~ **www.girlsinc.org**

Girl Scouts of the USA is a leadership development organization for girls with girl and adult members worldwide ~ **www.girlscouts.org**

The Evoluer House is a non-profit organization that empowers girls by nurturing positive self-expression and personal development ~ **www.evoluerhouse.org**

Rosh Hodesh: It's a Girl Thing! offers a proactive, informal education program that uses Judaism to enrich the lives of girls ~ **www.roshhodesh.org**

WriteGirl is a nonprofit organization for high school girls centered on the craft of creative writing and empowerment through self-expression ~ **www.writegirl.org**

CHAPTER 4

Cupid Shuffle

"Never limit yourself because of others'
limited imagination; never limit others
because of your own limited imagination."

—Dr. Mae Jemison
Astronaut

When a cute guy is on the scene, it's on and popping. What? Don't we fall for those pretty eyes? If he has a gorgeous smile, we're no good. Throw in a nice ride, and it's over.

Our hearts go pitter-patter. And our heads stop thinking properly. Sometimes we lose our right minds. Next thing you know, Crazy is our middle name. Maybe you've been there?

Girl, don't be ashamed. I bet most of us have been there. Many of us have made mistakes when it comes to L-O-V-E. All we can do is pick up our cracked faces from the floor. Put on some mascara and a coat of lip gloss, and keep smiling. So let's pause before we put ourselves out there again. Think about how we can avoid other car crashes and collisions as we ride along the freeway of love.

WHAT IS THIS?

First things first, let's define some terms. What's going on here? What's happening? Maybe it's easier to ask, "Who is he?" Is he a friend, a boy-friend, a booty-call, a hook-up or what?

The Friend Maybe you've known him a while. He's cool. You're comfortable with him. You can talk to him. And he's honest and real with you. You can chill with him, with no strings attached. He cares more about you than about getting to first base.

The BoyFriend You two are an item. It's legit. He introduces you as his girlfriend to his people. He calls you often. He spends quality time with you. He makes you feel special. You do the same for him. You both have a commitment to each other.

The HookUp He's kinda into you. But he may be playing the field. He just wants to kick it. And that's when he has time. You might really like him. But you don't really know where things stand.

The BootyCall He's some dude you know. He doesn't take you out. He makes a habit of contacting you at some disrespectful hour of the night. He only has one thing on his mind. It's usually physical. He has no intention to get to know how wonderful a person you are.

Sometimes we have our own version of where things stand. The real question is: Does it match up with his? Hey, it's your right to figure out what you want from the relationship. I mean really give it some thought. And then ask yourself how you feel about him and the situation.

A good move is to be upfront. Let that guy know what kind of relationship you want. You may not even be interested or ready for a relationship at the time. Let him know that, too. As long as you're clear, things should be fine.

DISSECTING GUYS

Many relationships start with a friendship. I'm not going to lie, it can seem like a challenge to get to know a guy better. It takes time to get to know a person. But the good thing is that many guys love getting attention from girls.

So GirlFriend, this mission is possible. We want to see what this guy's all about. We want to understand how his mind works. We want to know how he operates. What do you think of his intentions?

1. Talk to the guy who's been on your radar. Listen to what he has to say about himself.

2. Get to know his friends. Try to get in with his friend's girlfriends. Then you can hang around him in a group.

3. What's he into? Find out his hobbies, interests, or favorite sports so you can have something to discuss.

4. Ask him to do something that's fun for both of you. It can be a group thing or just you two. It's up to you.

ESSENTIAL THINGS

You've heard the phrase, "Talk is cheap." That's not the case when it comes to getting to know someone. Good conversation is priceless when you're dating. It makes you more at ease. And it gives you the freedom to be yourself.

So here are some questions to get down to the nitty-gritty.

• What are your plans for the future?

• What are your parents and your family like?

• What are your favorite songs, movies, and books?

- What's your idea of a perfect girl?

- What makes you tick? Smile? Scared? Proud?

OK, it's not like this is a job interview. You're not trying to find out everything on the first date. Give the guy a chance to warm up to you. You want him to be able to trust you, too. So shooting him with a bunch of questions at once is not smooth. You've got to be subtle, GirlFriend. You know how we do.

LET'S JUST BE FRIENDS

It's cold-blooded to tell the guy that you're just not into him. I mean, how would we feel if a guy said that to us? Give these a shot:

- I'm enjoying flying solo right now. I'm only accepting applications for friendship at the moment.

- We'd make a crappy couple. I know you too well. We'd drive each other mad.

- I'm kinda involved with someone right now. I just want to see where it is heading.

THE NEXT STEP

So you're into him. You doodle his name on your notebook. We get it. He's the one. Now the question becomes, where do you go from here? Try to keep your head in your heart's decision.

Keep this in mind: Sex does not equal love. Boys often think about getting physical. Girls have more emotional feelings. This can be a dangerous mix for any young girl who is crazy in love.

What Is Sex?

Having sexual relations with another person—such as oral, anal, or vaginal intercourse.

SEX TERMS

- **Oral Sex** Using the mouth to stimulate genitals

- **Anal Sex/Intercourse** Inserting the penis in the anus

- **Vaginal Sex/Intercourse** Inserting the penis in the vagina

- **Making Out** Kissing and touching for a long period of time

- **Abstinence** Refraining from sexual activities

STD TERMS

- **STD** Sexually transmitted diseases also called sexually transmitted infections (STIs). They're spread through sexual behavior. Some are also spread through skin-to-skin contact, or blood, semen, or vaginal fluids.

- **HIV** The Human Immunodeficiency Virus that causes AIDS. It weakens the immune system so it can't fight off infections. The virus is transmitted through blood, semen, vaginal fluids, or breast milk.

- **AIDS** The Acquired Immunodeficiency Syndrome (AIDS) is caused by the Human Immunodeficiency Virus (HIV). AIDS is an infection that results from a weakened immune system.

- **SAFER SEX** Being responsible about sex means reducing your chances of getting or spreading a sexually transmitted disease or becoming pregnant.

SAFETY TIPS

1. Know about STDs and pregnancy, using latex barriers like condoms and dental dams

2. Limit your number of partners

3. Get tested for STDs on a regular basis

"Safer sex" means that there are effective ways to reduce these risks of disease. But no sex is completely "safe" or risk-free unless you aren't having any sex at all.

For more terms, check the end of this chapter for a glossary.

The Waiting Game

GirlFriend, your body is so special. As for me, I always thought I was too valuable to be passed around. My mom would say to me, "Don't just lay up with any old body." In case no one has ever told you that, I'm telling you now. You're actually a priceless gem. Believe that!

So let's be straight up. Virginity is not corny the way some teens try to make it sound. If you do decide to give it away, make sure you don't feel like you are paying a price.

Sometimes guys struggle with waiting around. It's almost like they can go someplace else and get it in a casual relationship. But if he pressures you or expects it before you're ready, let him go. You wouldn't want him anyway, GirlFriend.

Before you make any decisions, just ask yourself:

- Why am I doing this?
- Who benefits?
- What are the consequences?
- How would I feel if my loved ones knew?
- What's the worst thing that could happen?
- What would I do if that worst thing did happen?

THE SEX TALK

DivaGirl asked former U.S. Surgeon General
Dr. Joycelyn Elders what she wants teens to know
about sex. Here's what she had to say:

- We are sexual beings from birth to death.

- Sex is sex—whether it's vaginal, anal, or oral.
  Consider the three Ps: pleasure, procreation,
  and protection. We can't have pleasure if we're
  worried about getting pregnant, catching an
  STD disease, or destroying our values.

- Girls need to be able to communicate their
  thoughts about sex with their partner. They
  should discuss prevention strategies and contra-
  ceptives. They should discuss foreplay and the
  relationship.

- If you're going to have sex, think about it. Plan it.
  And make sure it's something you want to do.

- Never have impulsive sex. Never have sex if
  you're using drugs or alcohol.

- Hormonal methods, such as birth control pills, do
  not protect against sexually transmitted infections. You need a barrier of protection: You must
  use a latex condom.

- Yes, condoms do break. It's true. But the vows of abstinence break far more easily. Never leave home without a condom in your purse.

- You should never be touched in places you don't want to be touched. Sex should be consensual. If sex happens against your will, it is rape. And it should be reported immediately to authorities.

- If you can't control your reproduction, you can't control your life. You must be sexually abstinent until you are ready to be sexually active.

STD Stats

- Statistics show one in four girls had an STD in 2008.

- Nearly half of African-American teen girls (48 percent) were infected with an STD in 2008, compared to 20 percent of white teens. And among young women, African Americans 15 to 24 years of age had the highest rates of chlamydia and gonorrhea in 2009.

Source: Centers for Disease Control and Prevention
2008 Study and 2009 National Surveillance Data
www.cdc.gov/std/stats09/adol.htm

R-E-S-P-E-C-T

What makes a relationship healthy? HoneyGirl, take it from me. If something is broken and can't be fixed, you might just need to toss it. But some things are worth keeping. Look for these signs to see if your relationship is a keeper.

Respect: Does he value your comfort zone? Do you know his boundaries? Respect has to go both ways.

Trust: Healthy relationships are built on trust. It's believing a person won't dog you out. You know they'll do right by you, even when you're not looking.

Truth: Being straight-up can save a lot of time and trouble. Lying can lead to more lying. And lies usually come to the surface. Dishonesty ruins trust.

Support: Have your partner's back. Sometimes we need reassurance and reality checks. You want to know that person will be there in good times and in bad.

Reciprocity: Reciprocity is key. It's all about the give and take. You don't have to keep score. But you both should have an equal hand in making plans and decisions.

Separate Identities: Keep your own life. Don't get lost in his world. Still remain close to your friends and family. And continue those activities that kept you busy before.

Dialogue: If you've got something to say, say it. Don't keep it bottled up. Try to find a nice way to put it. Or soften the blow by writing a note about what's on your mind.

CUPID COPS:

- You have the right to feel safe and secure at all times

- You have the right to say "no" to sex, no questions asked

- You have the right to have some me-time

- You have the right to bounce whenever you please

- You have the right to be respected

TIME TO ROLL

Hey GirlFriend, you can be in an abusive relationship without him putting a finger on you. Watch for these warning signs. He ...

- Blames you for all his problems.

- Tells you he can't live without you.

- Breaks or hits things to intimidate you.

- Threatens to hurt himself or others if you break up.

- Acts jealous if you to speak to certain people.

- Pressures you into sexual favors with "if you really loved me …"

- Humiliates you in public and belittles your opinions.

- Taps you in a playful way, but it just doesn't seem right.

- Has severe mood swings, sour moods, or a bad temper.

- Treats you like property rather than a person he values.

- Gets aggressive or abusive toward inanimate objects or animals.

- Forces you to choose between being with him or your friends.

- Uses or owns weapons or has a history of violence and fighting.

- Blows issues way out of proportion.

- Disrespects his mother or mistreats his parents.

If you answered "yes" to even one of these signs, talk with someone for advice. Or check out **www.loveisrespect.org**. If you need immediate help, contact the National Dating Abuse Helpline 1-866-331-9474 or 1-866-331-8453 (TTY).

A good sign: Does he hold the door open for you? This says a lot about him.

Dr. Susan Bartell
Teen Psychologist and Director of www.4healthygirls.com

TOP FIVE RULES FOR SURVIVING A BREAKUP

1. You deserve the BEST relationship possible! If this one isn't great, breaking up is the right thing to do! You will find another relationship when the time is right. DON'T stay with a guy just because you don't want to be alone.

2. NO second chances for a guy that is verbally, emotionally, or physically abusive.

3. Take a break from guys while you get over it— not even hook-ups or booty calls (with the break-up guy or anyone else). Wait about one week for every month you dated. And don't bounce right into another relationship.

4. Focus on what was great about the relationship, and what wasn't. When you are ready to move on, look for a guy who has the positives, but NOT the negatives.

5. Don't drown your sorrows. Stay away from alcohol, drugs, overeating, or any other self-destructive behaviors. Instead, get support from friends and family. Sharing how you feel will help you feel better faster, so don't keep it to yourself.

Just Like You

* Dominique, 15

Q: "How can I keep my boyfriend interested if I am not ready to have sex?"

Dr. Tiffany D. Sanders
Licensed Psychologist and Certified School Psychologist

A: "A lot of girls feel pressure to have sex or 'to put out' with their boyfriends in order to keep them interested. This type of pressure comes from a variety of sources that include from within themselves, their boyfriends, and popular culture, such as listening to sexually explicit music lyrics. Teenagers must realize that sex will not keep their boyfriend interested in the relationships—either he likes you for who you are or he does not. When you start to feel that he is only interested in you in order to have sex, that's a red flag to exit to the left! He should generally like you for your personality, character, intelligence, common interests, and values. His interest in you should be maintained by enjoying spending quality time dating you, going to the movies, and by the mere fact that you like to do things he finds enjoyable, such as watching sports, playing video games, or working out. Additionally, his interest in you should be maintained because he sees you as a friend who does not crowd his space, respects his time hanging out with the boys, and offers support to him when he faces a difficult

moment in his life. If you do all of the above and more and he's not interested in being your boyfriend unless you have sex, then recognize that he is not the boyfriend for you and walk away holding your head up high. The right guy is out there for you, and he will recognize you for your worth and not for what sexual favors he can gain from you."

* Megan, 16

Q: "How do I know if I am a lesbian?"

Judith R. Peters
M.B.A., H.H.S.A., HIV Pre-Post Test Counselor, Health Educator

A: "Many pre-teens and teens don't really know if they are a lesbian or not because they are not sexually active. As teenagers, so many young people start to realize their urges and sexual attractions, sometimes not knowing what to do or who to talk to. Many feel they can't discuss their feelings with parents, siblings nor school friends. When you find you're attracted to or dream about Hannah Montana, Taylor Swift, or Selena Gomez instead of Justin Beiber or Usher then you may indeed be a lesbian, a same-gender loving person. Look for an ally or Gay-Straight Alliance in your school or community. It's good to speak with teens and other women who can help shed light on the urges and feelings that start emerging as one grows up!"

Check It Out

Amplify Your Voice: This is the online home of Youth Action Network of Advocates ~ **www.amplify yourvoice.org**

I Wanna Know: This is a useful teen-centered website of the American Social Health Association ~ **www.iwannaknow.org**

Teen Wire: Visit Planned Parenthood's Teen Talk site ~ **www.teenwire.com**

Scarlet Teen: It offers sex education for teens in the real world ~ **www.scarleteen.com**

Sex, Etc.: This is a website that is written by teens, for teens, on sexual health issues ~ **www.sexetc.org**

Where To Go For Help?

Educate yourself, friends, and family about HIV/AIDS and what you can do to protect yourself.

Black Aids Institute: This organization is geared toward addressing the AIDS epidemic in the Black community ~ **www.blackaids.org**

My Sistahs: This website offers information and support for women of color on sexual health issues ~ **www.amplifyyourvoice.org/mysistahs**

Center for Young Women's Health: This site has helpful information for teen girls as they enter womanhood ~ **www.youngwomenshealth.org**

Get tested for HIV. Even if you think you have low risk for HIV infection, get tested whenever you have a regular medical check-up. Or, to find a testing site near you, call 1-800-CDC-INFO (232-4636), visit: **www.hivtest.org**, or on your cell phone, text your zip code to **Know IT** (566948).

YOUR SPACE

Is your relationship pretty much on track? Be honest with yourself. Or, do you think it needs an overhaul? This is about you, Girl—having the healthy beautiful life you deserve.

Write down your thoughts or action plan right here:

_____

_____

_____

_____

_____

Sexual Terms

abortion
a medical procedure that terminates a pregnancy

acquaintance rape
when a person forces sex on someone he or she knows (date rape)

age of consent
the age a person can legally agree to have sex; it ranges between 14 and 18 years of age, depending on your state laws

bi-curious
when a person is sexually attracted to the other sex but has expressed thoughts in having a romantic relationship with someone of the same sex

birth control
any method of contraception used to prevent pregnancy, includes condoms, implants, injections, IUDs, pills, patches, rings, and shots

bisexual
when a person is attracted to people of the same sex and the other sex

blow job
when oral sex is performed on a male (giving head)

chickenhead
a degrading term for a girl known for giving blow jobs

come
to have an orgasm or ejaculation

consensual
when each person agrees to have sex without force or manipulation and understands the consequences

contraceptive
a barrier, behavior, medication, device, or surgical procedure that prevents pregnancy (birth control)

condom
a latex or non-latex sheath rolled over a penis to prevent semen from entering another's body and to protect the penis from infection; female condom is a polyurethane pouch inserted into the vagina

crabs
parasites called pubic lice that cause itching in areas covered by pubic hair and other body hair, most often transmitted sexually

cum
male semen or ejaculation; girls may also use this term to refer to their sexual fluids

date rape

when you're raped by a friend or a romantic partner; if you say no and you are forced, it's rape even if you've had sex with that person before (acquaintance rape)

date rape drug

illegal drugs that make you pass out so you can't mentally or physically move or resist sexual advances; often slipped into drinks at parties or on dates

dental dam

a thin piece of latex material used to cover a female's genitals during oral sex to reduce the risk of sexually transmitted infection; the only branded product approved by the FDA is the Sheer Glyde Dam

diaphragm

a dome-shaped rubber cup used with spermicide gel to prevent sperm from entering the uterus; it is 88%-94% effective at preventing pregnancy; does not protect against STI

dry sex

when people go through the motions of sex (rubbing bodies) without inserting a penis into a vagina or into any other body part

ejaculation
release of semen, which contains sperm, from the penis, usually during orgasm; some women ejaculate during orgasm when fluid sprays out of their urethra

fellatio
when oral sex is performed on a man

fingering
inserting a finger inside a woman's vagina or rubbing her clitoris, or inserting a finger into the anus

French kissing
when people kiss with their tongues in each other's mouth; this passes saliva back and forth; except for herpes, most STDs are not passed this way

genitals
sex organs of males and females; includes the opening to the vagina, labia and clitoris on a woman, and the penis and scrotum on a man

getting wet
when a woman is aroused and her vagina becomes moist

giving head
when oral sex is performed on a man

hand job
when people touch another person's vulva or penis to stimulate the genitals

hard on
when the penis becomes rigid from sexual excitement and stands away from the body (erection)

herpes simplex virus type 1
an infection that very commonly causes small, blister-like cold sores around the mouth; it can also infect the genitals and anus it can be transmitted sexually and non-sexually

herpes simplex virus type 2
an STI that most commonly causes sores around the genitals, anus, but can also infect the mouth; usually transmitted sexually, it can't be cured but can be treated; consult a doctor

incest
sex or sexual activity between people who are closely related; it's illegal

libido
sex drive; sexual desire

lubricant
a specially designed jelly or lotion used to reduce unwanted friction, chaffing, and discomfort during sex

masturbation
touching your own body for sexual arousal

ménage a trois
French expression that means three people
having sex together (threesome)

menstrual cycle
the time from the first day of one period to the first
day of the next period; in women of reproductive
age, about 15-44, it is the period in which the
lining of the uterus is shed whenever implantation
does not happen, followed by the re-growth of
the lining of the uterus in preparation for
implantation

menstruation
the flow of blood, fluid, and tissue out of the uterus
and through the vagina that usually lasts from 3 to
7 days — the first part of the monthly menstrual
cycle

molestation
unwanted sexual activity

mono/mononucleosis
an infection transmitted through saliva that causes
a sore throat, swollen glands, and low-grade fever
(the kissing disease)

orgasm
the climax of sexual excitement when all the
muscles that were tightened during sexual arousal
relax and cause a very pleasurable feeling

orgy
a sexual activity including many people (group sex)

outed
publicly disclosing the sexual orientation of another person

outercourse
sexual activity that does not include putting the penis in the vagina or anus

platonic
when you are friends and no sex or romance is involved

puberty
the process of an adolescent becoming an adult; it involves a lot of physical and emotional changes

pubic lice
a parasite in a person's pubic hair that causes itching; it can be spread through sexual contact and cured with anti-lice medicated shampoo

pulling out
when a guy pulls out his penis during sex before ejaculation; does not protect against STDs; not as reliable as condoms or many other methods of birth control; also called withdrawal

questioning
when someone isn't sure about his/her sexual identity

rape

forcing or threatening another person to have sex
— even if people know each other or are married
to each other; having sex with someone who is
mentally or physically unable to agree; it's a crime

semen

whitish, sticky fluid that is released from a man's
penis during ejaculation; contains millions of
sperm

sexual abuse

unwanted sexual advances; even if you know the
person, it's illegal

sexual assault

using force in sexual activity; that includes kissing,
touching, oral, anal, or vaginal sex; even if you
know the person, it's illegal

sexual intercourse

when a man's penis is inserted into a woman's
vagina or into an anus

slut/stud

a degrading word for a girl/guy who is known for
having too many sexual partners

smegma

a white, cheese-like, stinky substance that forms
under the foreskin; can be rinsed off with soap
and water

sodomy

a degrading and old-fashioned term for anal sex
or same-gender sex

sperm

male reproductive cells found in semen; fertilizes
the female egg; some men's bodies leak sperm
into their pre cum

statutory rape

when an older person has sex with someone
between 12 and 18 years old, depending on
individual state laws, this would be rape

train

when guys take turns having sex with a girl against
her will (gang rape)

trans

an umbrella term for anyone who is transgender,
transsexual, cross-dressing, transvestite, or who
doesn't fit into one gender category

transgender

when a person's gender identity does not match
his or her biological sex

urinary tract infection

a bacterial infection in the urethra; symptoms
include an urgent need to urinate often, a
burning sensation when urinating (bladder
infection)

vaginal discharge

(normal) fluid released from the vagina for cleaning purposes, the amount and texture varies at different times of the month; (abnormal) vaginal fluids that smell bad and/or irritate the vagina or vulva can be caused by sexually transmitted infection or bacterial overgrowth

vaginal lubrication

fluids that lubricate the vagina when a woman is sexually aroused

virgin

when a person has never had sex

—glossary terms edited by Planned Parenthood

CHAPTER 5

Bling & Thing$

"It's crucial to expand your vision
of who you are today to include
who you want to be tomorrow."

— Suze Orman
Twelve Steps to Wealth

This is how it's supposed to be. You have a brilliant plan. You find a way to make some money with your idea. And you end up on a talk show, telling the whole story. Don't laugh! That's what happened to Jasmine Lawrence, when she went on *Oprah*, and she was just 15. She was talking about how using harsh chemicals turned into a hair nightmare. She went on to talk about how she made her own products with natural ingredients and how it made her hair grow back. Now, she shares her beauty secrets with everyone. You can find her Eden BodyWorks line at Wal-Mart stores across the country.

Jasmine was on to something. Think about it: Teen girls really know how to break the bank on clothes, makeup, jewelry, electronics, music, gifts, food, activities, and whatnot. HoneyGirl, we can shop until they turn off the lights. And some of us still would be fumbling around in the dark. Seriously, if you add it up, girls probably have the buying power of a small country.

That's a whole lot of spending, you know. Is there any earning going on in this picture? Do your parents foot the bill to support your shopping habits? Or are you a girl who works hard for the money? If so, shout out to the hard-working girls.

And do you have those days when you look up and you can't figure out where all your money went? Snap! That's jacked up, isn't it? Some of us are rubbing two nickels together, while others are rubbing together two Benjamins. But all of us can benefit from managing our money wisely. As we get down to business, let's talk dream jobs, cash flow, and smart choices.

WORK FOR IT

First of all, you're going to get that job, WonderGirl. That's the message we ought to say to ourselves in the mirror. Or look, say whatever you need to say to help you think positive thoughts. And understand this: That job you get may be after dozens of interviews and many rejections. How do you land a job? Keep trying. Be persistent. Don't give up. You can do it!

RÉSUMÉ ROAD MAP

It's all right if you don't have 10 years experience since you're in high school. No sweat. You can still wow them with a résumé. You may be a first-time job seeker. Maybe all your gigs have been part-time. A résumé can be your gold pass. This is your chance to say, "I love doing _____ . I would be very good at this job because of my skills. These are my career goals: _____ _____ ."

TWO REASONS YOU SHOULD HAVE A RÉSUMÉ:

- It says a lot about your professionalism. It tells employers you have already put some effort into finding a job. That also says to them, "This person will put some energy into working at a job."

- It can showcase your talent and strengths. Talk about your activities and work ethic. Mention your house chores or volunteer work. What did you learn from those experiences?

Below is just one of many formats that you can use. The library and Internet have a ton of them.

SAMPLE RÉSUMÉ

JANESA DOE
1234 My Street, Anytown, New State 12345
home: 555.555.5555 • cell: 666.666.6666
email: janesadoe@youremail.com

EDUCATION
Central High School   2009 – Present
Anytown, New State

WORK EXPERIENCE
Curl Up & Dye Hair Salon   2010 – Present
Shop Assistant
   • Schedule appointments for hair stylist
   • Greet clients as they enter the salon
   • Provide customer service with a smile

VOLUNTEER EXPERIENCE
Reading Is the Bomb Literacy Program   2009 – 2010
Library Aide
      • Hosted a weekly storytelling hour for underprivileged children
      • Assisted the library staff with their things-to-do list

Never Give Up Community Center   2008 – 2009
Teen Leader
      • Led group activities for children in the after school-program
      • Chaperoned children on community center field trips

EXTRA CURRICULAR
      • Future Business Women of America, Secretary
      • Girl Scouts, Troop #310, Member
      • Anytown Dance Hi-Steppers, Dancer

ACHIEVEMENTS
      • Anytown Teen Essay Contest, 2nd Place   2010
      • Academic Honor Roll, Special Recognition   2009, 2010, 2011
      • Good Attendance Award, Special Recognition 2009, 2010, 2011

COMPUTER SKILLS
      • Proficient in Microsoft Word, PowerPoint and Internet Research

YOUR RÉSUMÉ

YOUR NAME
Street Address, City, State Zip Code

home: ---,---,---- • cell: ---,---,----

email: _____

EDUCATION

_____20?? – Present

_____

WORK EXPERIENCE

_____20?? – Present

* _____
* _____
* _____
* _____

VOLUNTEER EXPERIENCE

_____ 20?? – 20??

* _____
* _____
* _____
* _____

EXTRA CURRICULAR

* _____
* _____

ACHIEVEMENTS
* _____ 20??
* _____ 20??

COMPUTER SKILLS
* _____
* _____

DREAM GIG

Your résumé is together. Think about what you'd like to do. Are you a natural at baby-sitting? Checking for positions at after-school programs, daycare centers, or summer camps may be a good lead.

High school is a prime time to learn what you like—and what you don't. You can lay foundations to a career in medicine now. How about getting a job as a lab assistant? What about helping out at a community clinic? If you're into graphic design, apply to photocopy shops like Kinko's. Or you could be a production intern at a newspaper in your community.

How do you find out what you're good at doing? Ask yourself this question: What is interesting to me? What job would I do for free? If you can answer those questions, you may have just discovered your true passion. Can you imagine yourself doing this position one day? Jump on opportunities when they come your way. They may be just the experience you need to land your dream job. Now ask yourself these questions:

1. What is your dream job?

2. What are the daily duties and responsibilities for
   this career?

_____

_____

3. What skills and talent would you need to land a
   job like this?

_____

_____

4. What skill can you develop now to use in your
   ideal position?

_____

_____

JOB HUNT

You've heard the phrase, "It's not what you know,
it's who you know." To be honest, many jobs are
found through people you know or some kind of
referral. That's just a fact of life.

So you can put the word out that you're on the
hunt for a job. Next, tell the world and everyone
you know that you need a job. Tell your teachers,
guidance counselors, coaches, family, friends,
neighbors, and church members. Ask them for

help, and maybe somebody will have the hookup.

All right, now you've got your people looking out for you. You've got to hit the pavement, too, SuperGirl. Are you one of those mall hoppers? If so, Girl just hop to a store and ask if they're hiring. Fill out an application and hop on to the next one.

Online searches are the new way of looking for employment. So include the high-tech route as part of your job search. Visit sites that cater to teen job opportunities. And who-knows-what kind of gigs you can find on Facebook or Twitter.

You could always do like they did in the old days and call employment agencies. They're listed in the phonebook or online. Perhaps you may find that companies are looking to hire young high school students.

Do your own thing: Look what these DivaGirls did!

BLOWING UP
CEO: Amber Liggett
BIZ: Amber's Amazing Animal Balloons
AGE: 15
Amber had a knack and talent for balloon twisting. And now she's a hit on the party circuit.

How it all started: She began experimenting with balloons when she was just 9 years old. "I taught myself how to make different balloon shapes." Her mother noticed her gift and encouraged her to develop her skills and start her own business.

Her success: Now Amber's *Amazing Animal Balloons* is literally blowing up. Things really took off for Amber when she worked her balloon magic at a local festival in western Pennsylvania. Then bookings for private events started rolling in. "I was able to grow my company, one job at a time." She's received many awards for her entrepreneurial spirit. And it turns out, she's just as brilliant in the classroom. This star student has earned recognition for academic achievement from **President Bush** and **President Obama**.

Making it work: Amber does more than just make animals for her kiddie clients. She describes herself as very interactive and animated with the children. "I give off a positive feeling with them. I want them to have fun." While Amber likes to invest her time with her clients and her craft, she leaves the promotion and marketing side of the company to her mother.

Her future: Amber wants to expand her business with more employees and venture into face-painting and other party-entertaining activities. She's already taken her business on the road with events

in Hilton Head, South Carolina; Washington, D.C.; and Las Vegas, Nevada. But that's not enough for this budding CEO, who plans to take her company international.

Her advice to teens: Be positive and believe in yourself. Make a checklist of goals you want to accomplish. Keep everything organized. And always think bigger.

~ **www.ambersballoons.weebly.com**

DANCING FEAT
CEO: Amiya Alexander
BIZ: Amiya's Mobile Dance Academy
AGE: 13

Amiya took her dance skills and a big pink bus on the road.

How it all started: "I've been dancing for 10 years," says Amiya who's trained in ballet, jazz, modern, salsa, meringue, and hip hop. "I studied at Debbie Allen Dance Camp, and I was a dancer for the Detroit Pistons for three years." Amiya says starting a dance studio on wheels came to her in a dream. "My mom went out and bought a used school bus and we had it painted pink." Once the seats were removed from the 52-passenger coach, it was tricked out with hardwood floors, a ballet bar, and mirrors. Now Amiya's Mobile Dance Academy can accommodate up to 12 young students.

Making it work: She teaches dance lessons to children in under-served, urban areas. Amiya usually works on the weekends; birthday parties are her big draw. "We also give lessons in the schools and daycare centers." If Amiya is busy with homework or school activities, she has one of three instructors step in to take her class. Her mother insists that school comes first with this dancing machine. "If my grades drop, I'm not allowed to teach that week."

Her success: She's the media darling in Detroit with features on TV and in newspapers. But she defines her success as being able to share her talent with others. "My students are happy. I'm having fun and everything is going well."

Her future: Her plans are to start a franchise of dance bus studios and a performing arts center that showcases music, dance, and theater. And then she's off to Harvard Medical School to study obstetrics or plastic surgery.

Her advice to teens: "What you put into it is what you get out of it," is something she says her mother always tells her. "It's a blessing that I'm able to do this. Believe in God first. Believe in yourself, and everything will work out." ~
www.amiyasdancebus.com

ROCK STAR

CEO: Bridgeja' Baker
BIZ: Creative Jewelry by Bridgeja'
AGE: 14

Bridgeja' enjoyed just wearing jewelry until she explored her creative side and decided to design her own line.

How it all started: Bridgeja' had an emergency with her braces, so her father promised to take her shopping after an orthodontist appointment. They decided to check out a bead shop next door to her doctor's office. "The salespeople started telling me about classes where I could learn to make jewelry," says Bridgeja'. She ended up taking 30 courses. She was fascinated with pairing different shapes and patterns with gemstones and crystals. When Bridgeja' was only 10 years old, she took some necklaces, bracelets, and earrings to a jewelry show at the home of a family friend. "I made $1,107." That's when she knew she had to go into business for herself.

Making it work: She got a name, a logo, a website, and a lawyer and got incorporated. Her mom serves as her marketing representative. And her father, who has no official title, pitches in as well.

Her success: Creative Jewelry by Bridgeja' is featured on her website and in boutiques around

New Orleans. And the teen accessories designer is usually on hand at various jewelry shows and expos around Louisiana, like the Essence Music Festival. Bridgeja' even sent her jewels to Fashionista-in-Chief **Michelle Obama**. "I received a letter from the White House saying I was being considered as the First Lady's jewelry designer."

Her future: "I'd like to be a pharmacist," says Bridgeja', who adds that science is her best subject. "I'd like to open my own pharmacy and have my jewelry sold there."

Her advice to teens: "Don't ever let anyone tell you that you can't do something. Just reach for your goals. Give back and donate to others." ~ **www.creative jewelrybybridgeja.com**

INTERVIEW REVIEW

So you've got your eye on a position. They're impressed with your résumé. Now it's time for your face-to-face. You're off to a good start. Here are some tips so you don't mess it up.

Be on Time: Please, whatever you do, don't be late. First impressions can last forever. Don't give them a reason to give your job to somebody else. In fact, to be safe, get there 10 to 15 minutes early. That gives you time to catch your breath and calm those nerves.

Dress for Success: You can be a little casual. The jeans and T-shirt don't cut it, though. Check the "Style Star" chapter for what works and what doesn't for the interview. A tailored top and skirt are always presentable. If you're applying at a company or a prestigious internship, break out the suit.

Do Your Homework: Confidence will shine through if you know a little something about the company and/or position. Let them know you've done some research. And if you really want to stand out, come prepared to ask your own questions.

You May Hear This Question: *Will you tell us a little about yourself?* This is the perfect question for you. You can slip in something about your skills, accomplishments, and abilities. They may want to know your goals, too. Remember to tell them how much you'd love working there. You might also be asked questions like these:

What are your strengths/weaknesses?

_____

_____

What are some of your extracurricular activities?

_____

_____

Why do you want to work for us?

_____

_____

SAVING TIPS

Pay Yourself First: Save a little from each paycheck or allowance. Even if you save just $10, it's worth it. You can open a savings account at a bank. Or you can put away your money in a piggybank.

Avoid Compulsive Purchases: Don't buy things you really don't need. When you shop, have your list with you. At least you can keep a mental one. But stick with it. If you see something you've just got to have, put it on your list for next time. If it's still there your next visit, that means it was meant to be.

Eat at Home: Eating out can be expensive. Eat some oatmeal for breakfast instead of Krispy Kreme. Pack a turkey sandwich instead of having that Whopper. And carry some snacks from home in case you get the munchies. Another tip for your wallet and your waistline? Water is cheaper than Coke or Snapple.

Better Shop Around: Get in the habit of doing price comparisons. We feel cheated when we've overpaid for something. Browse first and do a little research online or as you window shop. You never know, you may be able to get a store to match competitors' prices.

KEEP A BUDGET

Budgeting your money is a brilliant way of taking charge of your finances. You can write it down or type it up. Keep track of what's coming in. And then keep up with what's going out. And if you have to, pull out that calculator.

Your income should be higher than your expenses. The experts warn us: Spend less than you earn. Yeah, it's easier said than done. But a budget will help to keep you honest ... with yourself.

FREE FUN

Hey, it happens. Sometimes your cash flow gets mighty low. Just a few tweaks here and there in your social calendar will hold you over. Here are some free and fun things to do in the meantime ...

Luxuriate with your girls. Throw a homemade spa day. Pull out the mani-pedi products or skin-care treatments. Then invite some friends over to enjoy the pamper-fest.

Giving back makes you feel good on the inside. Volunteer at the Salvation Army. Or you can help out at a homeless shelter. This is also a résumé-builder.

Treat your room to a makeover. Transform it into your own private getaway. Decorate it with your favorite trinkets and everything that reflects who you are. A clean room can be an instant mood-lifter.

Take a stroll down memory lane. Reach out to an old friend on a social networking site. Or you can just pick up the phone, if you have the number. Reconnecting can be just what you've been missing.

Check your city guide. See what free festivals, shows, and museum exhibits are going on this month. Open your mind and try something new.

Just Like You

* Jayson, 16

Q: "What healthy saving/spending habits should I be thinking about at my age?"

Dr. Boyce Watkins

Finance Professor, Syracuse University and Founder of Your Black World

A: "As a teen, your thoughts about money should be on understanding its power. Money has power to change the world, and it certainly has power to change our lives. But most of us give away all of our power at the mall buying things that are going to be of little to no value to us in a very short period of time.

As you learn to understand the power of money, you can start by appreciating the idea of saving and investing, rather than spending and consuming. A person who thinks like a saver will never be broke, but a person who thinks like a spender will always have nothing. Also, it is important to let go of the hip-hop culture that tells us that your value as a human being is measured by the cost of your shoes, or the diamonds on your neck. Your value is determined by who are you, what you stand for, and being the best person you can be.

Don't let money define you."

Tina Wells

CEO and Founder of Buzz Marketing Group, who made her first million by age 26, also has a response for Jayson:

A: "It's never too early to start healthy saving/spending habits! First, make sure you're saving 10% of the money you receive. This includes gifts from parents and grandparents, money earned from a part-time job, and money from any other source. Also, try to save all of your change! Those quarters and dimes can add up, and you can use that cash for a major purchase. Finally, only buy what you can afford. There's no better feeling than purchasing something you love, and not having to worry about owing someone else for it. If something is too expensive, you can always save toward it."

Take It To The Street

Want to see exactly where your money goes? Try this ... keep receipts for one week to see what you purchased. Plug the numbers in on this chart.

YOUR WEEKLY EXPENSES

Category	Amount
EXPENSES:	
Savings	
Savings Account	
Bills	
Taxes - From Paycheck	
Utilities Electric, Cell Phone, etc.	
Groceries/Snacks	
Car	
Car Payment/Gasoline	
Bus or Taxi Fare	
Shopping	
Clothes	
Other Shopping	
Fun	
Movies, Parties, Outings, etc.	
Other Expenses	
EXPENSES TOTAL	

CHECK IT OUT

MyMoney.gov has money management advice for teens, on saving, spending, and borrowing money, and keeping your money in a financial institution ~ **www.mymoney.gov/content/money-management-teens.html**

The Mint provides practical advice for teens to manage their money ~ **www.themint.org**

CHAPTER 6

Holla!

"It doesn't matter what people call you.
What matters is what you answer to."

—Everybody's Grandma
Wise Old Saying

Whether we know it or not, we pretty much are constantly sending out messages. People tend to judge us by our spoken language—and our body language. Sometimes we get so caught up starring in our own drama, the rest of world can't even figure out what we're trying to say.

Case in point: Many watch the hot mess of *Reality TV Shows Gone Wrong* as one girl after another acts a plum fool. Even when we turn off the TV, those horrendous images of women clowning themselves continue to haunt us until the next episode.

Then, when we think it's safe to turn the TV back on, the producers have the nerve to air a senseless spinoff. Come on now. We hear some words and see some moves we've never seen before. Does anybody stop and ask herself, "What message am I sending the world?"

You know how it is when you're in a bad mood. You might just snap on someone. Maybe you didn't even realize that you snapped. What was on the inside can come out through your words or your actions, MissGirl. It doesn't matter if you're mousy or mouthy. You might stand or slump. This kind of stuff is communicating things about who you are.

I say this to say, Girl, you're not invisible—no matter how invisible you may sometimes feel. And when people see you, it's not just about what you're wearing that gets noticed, but the whole package. That's why it's good to pay attention to your overall style, your attitude, what you say, and how you say it.

Does everything have a season? Yes! I learned this early on. Even if you want to come across like you're "keeping it real." Keeping it real doesn't mean keeping it real ignorant. There's a time to play—and there's a time to work. There's a time to be down—and there's a time to switch it up and sparkle. You've just got to know the occasion.

Why? You ask. I believe every girl is placed on this earth to accomplish something remarkable, something only she could do. You've got to be ready for your big break. There might come a time for you to land that cool gig. Perhaps you'll meet a record label executive for an internship. You may even have to represent your classmates at the White House. You best bring your A-Game.

Take it from me, the girl who went from a group home to work alongside fashion's elite. You never know, DivaGirls. Your wildest dreams could become a reality when you least expect it. Are you ready to make them happen? Are you ready to represent? If you're not, that's OK. You've got some time to get it together, but the sooner the better.

My wish for you is to be ready—the world really is yours for the taking. It really is!

Body Talk

Body language is what you say through your motions, movements and mannerisms: You know, the head jerking, teeth sucking, eye rolling. It's also looking at somebody like they have the cooties.

Say What?

A DivaGirl's got to be hip to what she's telling people—even when she's being quiet. Here's her checklist:

EYE CONTACT

- Maintain good eye contact to show respect and interest in what others have to say. Too much eye contact may spook people. Too little eye contact might make you seem unsure.

- Share equal eye contact if you're speaking to people in a group. That's a good way to engage everyone in the conversation.

- Blink occasionally. You don't want to be staring or gritting on others. And a seldom head nod helps to show you're paying attention.

POSTURE

- Stand up tall, be proud, show confidence. No need to hunch your body to make yourself seem small.

- Sit up straight. Don't slouch. Shoulders should be down and relaxed. People will believe what you're saying.

- Keep your head straight up. Keep your eyes at eye-level. Show people you're self assured.

HANDS/ARMS

- Putting your hand in front of your mouth shows that you're timid.

- Rubbing your nose, eyes, ears, head, or neck show signs of doubt.

- Fiddling with jewelry makes you seem bored or nervous.

- Crossing your arms looks defensive.

MOUTH/LIPS

- Smile when you're introduced to some one. But a plastered smile on your face may seem phony.

- Laugh when someone says something funny. But don't laugh at your own jokes. It makes you seem nervous and even corny.

- Relax your lips. We twist our lips when we have something angry to say.

SLANG SLINGIN'

Why you be talkin' like that? We know about your ever-changing vocabulary of code words. Your language can be colorful, creative, and even helpful in some settings. But slang, or should we call it slingin' slang, can be a foreign language to people outside your circle.

You know parents don't understand it. That's why I used to speak in Pig Latin, like this: "eetmay ouyay atway eena's day ousehay 9 pmay." I just told my girl: "Meet you at Deena's house 9 pm." LOL!

That was a hoot then. These days a girl has to be bilingual. I mean, you have to be able to communicate with all kinds of people. Think about ways to amp up your lingo. That way, you can express what you want to say. And people can actually understand you.

GIFT FOR GAB

- Learn a fresh new word each week. Use it in your everyday vocabulary.

- Keep a thesaurus handy. Find alternatives for words you always use.

- Learn another language, like Spanish. French is a hip language, too.

- Save street slang for the street. That's a foreign language in the real world.

Just in case, someone might say you talk too proper. Don't be ashamed because you know how to speak. Good communication skills will take you further than you can imagine, no matter how somebody tries to flip it. Look at **Lisa Ling** and **Wendy Williams**. They took their gifts for good gab all the way to the bank.

GOSSIP GIRL

We might all be guilty of this. But some girls could be arrested for how they crack on other people. They get caught up in spreading other people's business around town. They don't think about the downside. Gossip can seem like fun until you're the target of the gossip.

COMMON GOSSIP STARTERS:

- I heard her parents are illegal immigrants.

- I heard she's dating a drug dealer.

- I heard she is in all those smart-girl classes.

- I heard she is in the slow class.

- I heard she just got out of juvy.

- I heard she's playing three different dudes.

- I heard she's had two abortions.

See, this is how rumors get started. If you and or your girls begin a conversation with these sentences, nothing good will come out it.

You're The Target?

It happens to the best of us. People have been running their mouths. Your business is out on the street. And it's making people look at you sideways. Sometimes it doesn't matter if the rumors are even true. And you're trying to figure out who said what. Now you feel like you can't trust anyone.

Don't confront the gossip. That could lead to a bloody blowout. It's not worth it. Just laugh it off. Then flip it. Say that you've heard just the opposite thing about yourself. Be cool and ignore it. Act more mature than the rumors circulating about you. And the rumors will usually die down. If things seem like they're about to spin out of control, you might want to tell your parents or an authority figure as soon as you can.

You're The Gossip?

It's easy to chime in about someone who's not there, adding your negative two cents to the pot. They're going to know who started flapping their lips first. Then what will they think of you? You'll have people thinking you're shady. If you say something about someone, you'll say something about anybody. That will be the message you're sending.

It wouldn't be so bad if people knew how to keep their mouths shut. But that's not how most of us operate. You know what happens when you tell someone to keep a secret? Before you can blink an eye, they end up telling the whole world.

Before you get ready to talk smack, stop yourself. Think, "Would I want someone saying that about me?" Try to put yourself in someone else's shoes. If what you're saying is hurtful to you, it will probably be hurtful to someone else.

It can be funny to see how people react to the stories you tell. But laughter at the expense of another person just ain't right. People might say they think you're funny, but they're probably really wondering why you feel the need to be downright mean.

Take a stand against gossip. Change the subject or dispute the rumor. You can break the cycle.

Ho! Ho! Oh No!

One of the fascinating gifts of being a teen is that you set the tone for what will be the next hip thing. Replacing those degrading terms like "bitch" or "ho" with more positive ones can be just as entertaining. Imagine how your friends will respond when you greet them like this: "Hey Angel!" "What's up, Scholar! " "See you later, Princess!" It's all in how you flip it. Those are real terms of endearment.

* Wanda, 17

Q: "Why do girls think it's cute to call each other a 'bitch' or a 'ho?' What could I tell them if I don't want to be called by those names?"

Beverly Bond
Founder of Black Girls Rock!

A: "Quite often, people try to give negative words positive appellations. However, when we consider the long history of words like 'bitch' or 'ho,' it becomes very difficult to defend the aforementioned behavior.

It's never cute or acceptable for girls to call each other outside of their names. The words 'bitch' and 'ho' are especially derogatory and have historically been used to disempower women and girls. Furthermore, a long lineage of female suffragists has committed their lives to making sure that women would no longer be subordinated or disenfranchised. Therefore, it is disrespectful and disappointing when girls use inflammatory language against one another.

When a young lady uses vulgar language to describe another girl, the action suggests a lack of self-respect and insinuates that the young lady does not value herself or her sister. Similarly, when women accept

negative labels, they also display an immense lack of self-dignity. The labels that we accept or reject play an important role in personal identity development. By accepting labels with negative connotations, one also accepts the history of disrespect, subjugation, pain, and slander that comes along with the language.

Lastly, those who choose to use derogatory words ultimately limit the circles that they can frequent. As these individuals mature, they will find that there are very few positive and successful people who will tolerate being called outside of their name or who will allow disrespectful discourse within their personal or professional social networks.

If you are ever in a situation where someone calls you a name that has a negative connotation, correct them immediately and let them know that being in your company is synonymous with having a line of mutual respect."

TAKE IT TO THE STREET

You can have a good time practicing your body language in front of a mirror.

Try to observe friends, role models, and celebrities you like who have great body language. Pick up positive mannerisms that work for you. Set aside a few minutes every day for three weeks to practice your new moves. By then it all might be something you do without even flinching.

YOUR SPACE

Now think about a time that you may have been mis-understood. Did the way you came off to someone have anything to do with it? Honestly … go ahead and journal about it here. Listen, some of us think we can do no wrong. But when you write it down and read what you wrote later, don't be surprised if you say, "What? I did that? Oh my goodness!"

CHAPTER 7

Act Like You Know

> "I don't think of myself as a poor
> deprived ghetto girl who made good.
> I think of myself as someone who from an
> early age knew I was responsible for myself,
> and I had to make good."
>
> —Oprah Winfrey
> *Media Mogul*

Here's the situation: You've been invited to an A-list event. This is your chance to shine and make connections. There will be all kinds of networking opportunities here. You know you want that big internship. Well, WonderGirl, this is the place to be and be seen. The guest list is a who's who in radio and television.

Of course you want to bring your girl, right? You roll up to the event. Who's the first person you see

145

standing just a few feet away? It's **Selena Gomez** looking too sharp. Your girlfriend, a newbie on the social circuit scene, starts talking all loud about how she can't stand this person and that person and how she's going to clock so and so.

You want to pretend like you don't know who she is, but you know that may really set her off. Little did you know her performance would be the talk of the event. And we don't mean in a good way. What would you do if this happened to you?

I would …

Try to talk to her about her attitude. Why?

_____

_____

Never invite her to another public event. Why?

_____

_____

Ex her off my friends list. Why?

_____

_____

Fill in the blank:

_____

_____

CONSIDER THIS

To be honest, sometimes, you have to draw the line. It's like we have to make wise decisions when it comes to career goals. What will help; what will hurt? On the real tip, I have friends ... I can dress them up, but I can't take them out because they just don't know how to act.

If I had to learn one thing: There's a way you act with your friends in the street. But in a professional setting, it's a whole different scenario.

You may want to go places in life and discover new things. Before you jet, it's a good idea to act like you know—no matter where you go.

Seriously, if the opportunity ever came to go to the United Nations for a dinner party, you wouldn't start a food fight. If you were in a quiet library, you wouldn't think about yelling across the room. You know you'll be kicked out. That's because every environment you enter will have its own set of unspoken rules.

I'll tell you, once you get down all the Ps and Qs, you'll probably have more fun when you're out and about. You could end up with all kinds of invites to go places, too. You could be that girl who people enjoy having around.

Etiquette! "Etti-What?"

Basically, etiquette means good manners. True that, the term "etiquette" may seem a little played out. But when it comes down to it, all it means is, "Do you know how to act, without acting out?" Because a girl needs to know how to handle herself, whether she's at a fancy event or chilling with her crew. If you're that girl with goals, etiquette is a term you ought to know and practice.

Home Training

Home training is another old-school term. You may not hear it too much unless it's from your grandma. But the meaning is basically the same: acting like you have some sense. Or, like my grandma would say: "Girl, you better not embarrass me out in public." God bless her, she just wanted to make sure that I was doing these things:

- Showing respect for elders

- Greeting people politely

- Carrying myself like a lady

- Watching my mouth

- Saying "thank you," "please," and "excuse me"

Here's the 411 to help you breeze through your social calendar with mad grace and style:

BASHES, SHINDIGS & RECEPTIONS

- Always RSVP (respond to say you're coming) if you want to go. Only bring a guest if the invite allows a plus one—not your celebrity-style entourage. The hosts prepare for a specific number of guests.

- Get the lowdown on the guest list and dress code from the host. This will give you an idea of what to wear and the type of affair you'll be attending.

- Get gorgeous from head to toe. You never know who you'll meet at these functions. You want to leave a good impression.

- Mix and mingle. You may not know a soul. You may be shy, so force yourself to say hello. Avoid hanging out at the refreshment table stuffing your face with cheese cubes.

MAKING SMALL TALK

For starters, it might help to bone up on some research before you attend nice events. Think about it. If you know something about the other guests, you'll have more to talk about. It wouldn't hurt to brush up on some current events, too. If you've got a minute, try to check out the latest news story of the day.

As you stroll the event, you may want to join an ongoing conversation. That's fine. If you see friendly faces and overhear an interesting discussion, wait around. Maybe you'll be invited to chime in.

Part of making great small talk is being a good listener. Generally, people love to talk. Remember to smile, nod, and throw in an "OMG" and a "Seriously?" to seem like you're into the conversation. Make good eye contact, and you could be a hit.

BREAKING THE ICE

Think of some basic questions you would ask another guest. Can't think of any? Check out these simple conversation starters, and then write your own questions below:

"What brings you to this event?"

"How do you know the host?"

"What is your line of work?"

_____

_____

_____

_____

How do you make a graceful exit? Think of some conversation enders when you want to cut things short. Here are my two favorites and then jot down your examples below.

"It was nice to meet you. Enjoy the rest of the evening."

"Do you have a business card so I can stay in touch?"

_____

_____

_____

_____

_____

CONVERSATION NO-NOS

Guess which three topics are off limits in social settings? Religion, politics, and money. Lots of etiquette coaches include sex on that list of inappropriate social conversations. A DivaGirl never wants to offend so she wants to avoid asking embarrassing personal questions like these:

"Have you had plastic surgery?"

"How much money do you make?"

"Dang, how old are you?"

NETWORKING & SCHMOOZING

Girl, this is when you've got to be ready to let your light shine and chat about you—your hobbies, favorite books, or music. Go grab your girlfriend; make her listen to your spiel. Find out what was her first impression of you. Ask her what she finds interesting about you. And have her give you some honest feedback.

Are you good with names? I'm not. But there are little tricks to remembering them. When you meet somebody new, actually listen to her name. Then say, "Nice to meet you, _____."
Repeating the name will help you remember.

A positive attitude is simply marvelous. It's also half the battle in acing any social situation. Go ahead, show your self-confidence, MissGirl. And be optimistic. And if you don't feel it, don't be ashamed to fake it—because the point is to act like you know and belong.

Go all out to talk to guests from different ages, ethnicities, and social backgrounds. Live a little! Step out of your comfort zone, because life is about going places and discovering new things.

STUMBLE? NO BIGGIE

Hey, it happens to the best and the brightest of us. Embarrassing moments can make us want to crawl in a hole. The only good thing about it is we tend to laugh about it later. OK, it may be years later. Look at it this way: You've got a funny story to tell at the next party. And believe it or not, most people will relate.

Keep this in mind the next time you take a slip. What does **Naomi Campbell** do when she trips on the catwalk? That diva has herself a good laugh. She gets up and keeps serving that runway. Now you know that's hot.

THANK YOUS!

It's always nice to show someone that you appreciate them. So when they show you kindness, show some love right back. You can start by writing thank-you notes. Send them to grandparents or other people who've helped you along the way. If you're the creative type, make your own stationery to say thanks. Or just buy a snazzy card.

Formal Table Setting

1. Napkin
2. Salad fork
3. Dinner fork
4. Fish fork
5. Dinner knife
6. Fish knife
7. Soup spoon

8. Bread & butter plate
9. Butter knife
10. Dessert fork, knife, spoon
11. Water glass
12. Red wine glass
13. White wine glass
14. Dinner plate

DINING OUT

You may be indulging at fried-rice joints or five-star bistros. Want to see how your table manners measure up? Take this quiz.

1. Something horrible-tasting is in your mouth. What do you do?

   A. Spit it on the plate and yell, "Gross!"

   B. Swallow and smile.

   C. Subtly push the food out of your mouth and into your napkin.

2. You have to belch, but it's going to sound like thunder. What do you do?

   A. Hold it in and hope it doesn't come out the other end.

   B. Let it out like there's no tomorrow.

   C. Excuse yourself or cover your mouth with your napkin and say, "Pardon me."

3. You want the server to refill your water. What do you do?

   A. Holler, "Yo Dude, can I get a refill?"

   B. Snap your fingers and yell, "Over here."

   C. Gracefully lift your index finger and ask politely.

Don't cheat, but you can find the answers in the Resource Guide.

TABLE 'TUDE

MissGirl, forget about memorizing the shapes and sizes of the different utensils, plates, and glasses. Follow one simple rule: Start with the outside utensils, set farthest away from your plate. Then with each new course, use the next utensil in the setting, moving inside toward your plate.

The next step is to identify the plates, glass, and the napkin so that you don't end up using your neighbor's items. The plate is right at the center. You have your glass to your right and the napkin and the bread plate to your left.

Still confused? Then just follow others. Even if you don't get it right, keep things moving peacefully. Quickly glance at your dinner mates and just follow their actions to pick the right silverware. Pretty soon this stuff will be second nature to you.

CHOW BELLA

Put your chi-chi poo-poo party skills to the test. Host a casual-chic, fine-dining experience with a three-course menu. Serve your guests appetizers: soup or salad. Then bring out the second course, which is your entrée. And end the meal on a sweet note with dessert.

Call about five other members of your crew. Tell them to dress to impress. Have everybody arrive early, and then put them to work. The challenge? See who can arrange their table setting correctly. Do they have the fork in the right place? Is their plate where it should be? The first one who gets it right gets a prize (that you bought earlier from the dollar store. Don't laugh! It's the perfect place to buy cute little door prizes.).

Here's what you'll be doing while you're getting your fine-dining experience on:

- Ask the guys to pull chairs out for the girls.

- Show guests how to place their napkins in their laps.

- Inform them how to pass the food.

- Demonstrate how to properly use their silverware.

- Chew with their mouths closed.

What to serve? Girl, get some takeout. Or it can be something as simple as:

- First course: onion soup or mixed-green salad

- Second course: chicken, veggies and baked potato or spaghetti and meatballs

- Third course: a fabulous cupcake or exotic ice cream

On The Town

Are you on your way to a **Justin Beiber** concert? You might be going to see *America's Best Dance Crew* tour. Or maybe you scored tickets to *The Lion King*. You don't want to miss a minute, so arrive on time.

If you're late, you might miss the best part. It's also a distraction to other audience members and the performers. And the bad part, sometimes the usher will seat you where they want you to sit. Or they may make you wait. That's no fun.

Intermission is the best time to leave your seat. The break is usually 15 minutes long. You can go grab a drink or a snack. That's also a good time to use the ladies room. And if you're cutting out early, that's the best time to exit.

You know you don't want to be sitting next to loud-mouth SheNayNay from *The Martin Lawrence Show*. You pay all that money for your ticket and you can't even hear the performance. So keep your conversations brief and to a whisper.

And if you're not sure when to clap, just wait until everyone else does and join in.

IN THE SPIRIT

Places of worship are welcoming, and they are for-giving places. At the same time, they are worthy of the highest respect. They may not represent your beliefs or religion. And that's perfectly fine. If you step foot in one though, keep in mind that they are sacred places. And their rules should be honored.

Whenever you visit a new church, never question what's happening. Sometimes people shout "Amen" and scream "Hallelujah," and there's a lot of kneeling and bowing. You're not there to criti-cize it. If you're curious, you can find out about the customs and rituals later.

Many churches invite you to come as you are. But you know some of us can put a whole new spin on that, right? So why not play it safe. Double-check that what you're wearing isn't too tight. If it's some-thing we'd sport to the club, try to save it for the club. And if you're torn between wearing pants or a skirt, you can always win with the skirt.

MissGirl, sometimes we're flashing the minister and we don't even know it. That's why we've got to keep our legs crossed at the ankles anytime we sit on the front row. You want to make sure your pri-vate business remains private. And follow that rule wherever you are, no matter what the event.

Meet U @ The Mall

The shopping mall is a teen girl's paradise. It's got clothes, cosmetics and, of course, the fellas … Hey! Sounds like a perfect way to spend a Saturday afternoon, huh?

Yeah, we're there to have a ball. We've still got to keep it classy, though. You know how it is. We're in a public place, after all. You could be there to hook up with your friends. You may be there to shop till you pass out.

While you're there, strive to be respectful to other shoppers. Carry yourself in a courteous manner. Show the mall cops that teens know how to act. You know security is just waiting to say something. Malls want people to shop and spend money. It's cool if you're there hanging out and not shopping. Just at least try to stay out of trouble.

The shopping mall can be a danger zone, so stay safe with these tips:

- Stay alert because predators hang out in the malls.

- Scout out the security stations in case you need to get to them quickly.

- Dress to stand out, not to shock and attract unwanted attention.

- Traveling with friends is a good defense. And remember a DivaGirl's safety code: "We came together, we leave together."

PUBLIC TRANSIT

We sometimes enjoy jamming to our MP3 player. Nothing wrong with that. But giving a free concert on mass transit can irritate the mess out of people—especially the elderly. So chill with the **Lady Gaga** sing-a-longs in public. We know you sound good, DreamGirl. But you probably sound even better in the shower.

And you know what it's like on a crowded bus. How many times have you seen this? All the seats are taken and a pregnant woman or person with a disability is standing. Go on and give up your seat. Consider that your good deed for the day.

CHECK IT OUT

Teen Manners: From Malls to Meals to Messaging and Beyond by Cindy P. Senning and Peggy Post

JUST LIKE YOU

* Raven, 14

Q: "Do you have any advice on how young girls should behave when they are out and about?"

Kenya Moore

Former Miss USA, Actress, Model, and Producer

A: "Young girls should always conduct themselves like ladies at all times. Ladies never get drunk or inebriated. Ladies never disobey their parents. Ladies respect their elders and authority figures. Ladies never act in an overtly sexual way. Ladies do not follow, they lead. And ladies do not have to be loud or boisterous to get attention. This is the wrong kind of attention.

Essentially, you teach people who you are and to respect you by demanding respect with your behavior. You should always be polite, kind, patient, pleasant, and respectful of others. Also, nonverbal communication speaks volumes as well.

People are constantly watching you even when you think they are not. This includes potential employers, teachers, someone who is on a scholarship board, parent's friends or even a potential mate, etc. So it is key to always treat people the way you want to be treated. But most importantly, be yourself. Be confident. Be you. And remember that you are unique. There is only one you."

CHAPTER 8

Tech Smartz

"I was born free.
I'm a cell phone hippie."

—Taylor Swift
The Diary of Me

Chatting, for some of us, can be a form of pure entertainment. Are you one of those girls who burn up the line for hours talking with your friends? It's funny how sometimes we might look up and wonder where all that time went.

I remember hearing my mother and aunts on the phone. It sounded like they were throwing a party. They were so colorful with their lingo. And they taught me how to put the "I" in "Girl*lll* …"

Those were the old days. Communication has changed a lot. And the tools of communication have changed even more. And now the language is new: Everything is abbreviated like OMG … LOL … BFF … XOXO.

In today's interactive world, we all try to be up on the latest gadgets—and lingo. While we're at it, we can take a moment to brush up on some cyber-etiquette, too. Because let's face it, we can get a little carried away sometimes.

Shooting the breeze via text message and cell phone is just not as harmless as it used to be. We live in different times from when two girlfriends could share a private conversation.

Now we don't know who's listening or who's watching. To be on the safe side, we should think about that before we open our mouth or go sending off that text. Let's go over some rules for playing this tech-savvy game. Here's the rundown on how to represent on the phone and online.

CALL ME

Diamonds may be a girl's best friend, but a blinged-out cell phone is today's accessory of choice. There's nothing wrong with being sassy-chic, especially if that cell is always glued to your ear.

If you're like some of us, it may be your prized possession, even if it's not dripping in rhinestones.

Cell phones are mad convenient. It's scary for us to think about our lives without them, isn't it? But we can't get too comfortable. This calling schedule may keep you on everyone's good side:

- We all need our beauty sleep, so wait until after 7 a.m. on weekdays to ring someone.

- On the weekends, some people like to sleep in a little later. So calling after 10 a.m. is considerate.

- At night, some people can't hang, so calling before 9 p.m. should be a safe bet.

- Calling during dinnertime is off limits. You know how it is when people are getting their grub on.

When you call a friend and someone in her family answers the phone, just introduce yourself: "Hi, this is Shana. May I please speak to Letitia?" And remember to say thanks! That's kinda like a simple word that reminds people how sweet you are.

- If you leave a message, be sure to leave your name, phone number, and reason for calling.

- Remember to speak slowly and clearly. Some messages are hard to understand. We strain our ears trying to make sense of them.

- On the safety tip, if you're home alone, that's not everybody's business. If the caller asks for someone who's not home, just take a message.

- If you dial the wrong number, just apologize and then hang up. Prank calls can be tempting when you're bored with friends. But they're annoying to others. And with the caller-ID technology today, it's just not a good move.

GREETINGS

We've all heard them. You make a call and hear a cute outgoing message on the voice mail. Or you may have heard a crazy greeting telling you to leave a message. Sometimes we're just expressing ourselves. But those greetings can say a lot about us, can't they?

If you're trying to up your professional game, let's think twice before recording these greetings:

"Hi, House of Beauty, this is Cutie! I'm into me right now, so leave a message."

"Hi! (long pause) Why aren't you saying anything now?"

DivaGirls can check out these helpful tips when greeting callers:

- Keep your greeting short and polite.

- Background music can be played out.

- Give them all the info they need if you're not available.

- Return your calls in a timely manner.

SAMPLE OUTGOING MESSAGE:

"This is (name). I'm unable to take your call at the moment. Please leave your name, phone number, and a brief message, and I will contact you as soon as possible. Thanks."

OK, some of us may need to spice it up just a little bit. But we can still be professional, right? Try recording your own outgoing message. Write down your script right here before you do it:

_____

_____

_____

_____

Now play it back. Let your family and friends listen. Get their opinion. Most people don't nail it on the first take. So re-record until you have a keeper. You know how to turn on that switch that says, "I'm all about the business."

Now you've got it, SuperGirl. In no time, you may be getting callbacks from prospective employers. That's why you want to come across as someone they'd be proud to hire.

CHECK THIS SCENARIO:

Imagine yourself trapped on a bus. Someone next to you is acting a clown on the cell phone. Maybe she's loud and ignorant. Every other word is a four-letter vulgarity. She's straight-up giving girls a bad name. People start to stare, and you hope she shuts up! But you don't want to start anything. You just shake your head and pray your stop comes up sooner rather than later.

Listening to some phone conversations can be plain-old embarrassing. Sometimes people don't consider who's around them. Somebody's grand-mother or innocent children could be listening. The same guidelines for talking on a regular telephone also apply to cell phone users. Here are some DivaGirl tips for cell phone manners in public:

- Nobody wants to hear you cursing up a storm, talking about your menstrual cramps, or fanta-sizing about intimate details with your boo. Save these topics for when you have more privacy.

- If there's bad reception, hang up and call them later. Don't ask if they can hear you 50 times like that's going to help you find a cell phone signal.

- Keep your phone conversations brief in public, unless you're alone.

- Chill with the personalized ring tones. Keep it classy. Keep it clean. In more professional settings, keep it on vibrate.

- And never text and drive. It's too dangerous.

OUT THERE

As they say in fashion, sometimes less is more. So how about we apply this advice to our online activities? Come on BabyGirl, can't we leave some things to the imagination?

You've heard of TMI. Ask yourself if having all your business out in the street is a good look. Think about it. Do you want people to know you on your terms or what may be traveling out there in cyberspace?

In this day and age, here's the reality: Once something goes viral, you have no control over it. We don't know where something will end up. We don't know who will see it.

OK, I can't lie, many of us have forwarded messages on to friends. When we do this we certainly aren't expecting the whole world to see these messages, are we? But actually, that can happen. You know how long it takes online content to travel? A matter of seconds. That means it can be around your school in a few minutes.

Guess what. Photos you send on your cell phone travel the same route? Yep, they can end up anywhere. Now knowing that, think about these two questions:

What would you do if your boyfriend wanted you to send him topless photos of yourself?

_____

_____

_____

_____

What would you do if those photos went viral?

_____

_____

_____

Once you push send, the whole world has the potential to see you at your most vulnerable state. They call it "sexting" when you send sexy photos to your boo on your cell phone. It's becoming a popular pastime for teens.

On a serious tip: It's illegal to send nude pictures of underage teens. That's called pornography. Even if you don't get arrested for sending those naughty photos, the embarrassment and humiliation could be just as devastating.

WHO'S THERE?

Would you believe that the average person lies about twice a day? Online, it's much easier to front and fib. As soon as we enter a chat room, we hide behind screen names and a cute avatar. We can create a whole new identity for ourselves like ##SEX MI ##, <<LuciiOuSz>>, and $$MuLa SuCca$$.

Sound familiar? To dust off an old saying, honesty is the best policy. Perhaps you've done it before, like giving a fake age. Yeah, it may be tempting trying to come off older than you are. Trying to act like an adult, though, can lead you into some adult, and sometimes dangerous, situations. So watch yourself!

Look at it like this. Honesty is different from telling all your business. Your private details are something precious. You can think of it that way before you go sharing contact information with anyone online.

Now this works both ways. You may encounter lots of shady characters on the Internet. Shifty eyes and body language are hard to see if you're not face-to-face. But here are some clues that may help:

- Watch for inconsistencies or contradictions with the info. When people are being shady, they can't keep their stories straight.

- If people are being vague, be aware. People will share details about themselves when they really want to get to know you.

- Say you really connect with someone online. If they even think of asking you for money, that's a red flag. So run for the hills.

- That strange or funny feeling you get about some people, that's your intuition talking. Take it as a sign that something is up.
  *And always ask plenty of questions.

Virtual Eternity

What goes online, stays online. Your online profile can be viewed by anyone, including future employers, college admissions officers and potential boyfriends. Are you comfortable with what yours says about you?

Social Sites

If you want to join a social network like Facebook, MySpace, or Twitter, then there are some things you need to do to protect yourself.

- Be careful who you include on your friends list. Make sure you know them.

- Don't do or say anything online that you wouldn't do or say offline.

- Check your friends' comments and photos to make sure they're protecting your privacy.

- If you wouldn't want your parents to see it, don't post it. Keep it for your diary.

Cyber Circles

Technology is an amazing thing. It has really changed the way we communicate with each other. But a cell phone can't high-five you and tell you everything's going to be OK. And your laptop can't hold your hand and wipe away your tears. Machines can't replace our friends, even though we may spend more time online than we do with actual people.

Tech Junkie?

Come on, where would we be without social networks, sharing details about every moment of our lives? Go ahead. Write it down here: I would be ...

If you have to define your digital life, how would you describe it?

_____

_____

_____

Or would you say your digital life defines who you are? Yes _____ No_____

How's this for a cyber check? If you're too obsessed living your life online, it's time you come back to the real world. Admitting you have a problem is your first step toward recovery:

You may be a tech junkie …

- If you prefer texting to human interaction, you've got online fever.

- If you speak in terms of LOL, OMG, and TTYL, you need to just spell it out.

- If you constantly sneak away from people to check your Blackberry, shame on you.

- If you skip showers, miss meals, and lose sleep, you've got a problem.

Just Like You

* Clem, 13

Q: "My girlfriends keep telling me to send sexy pictures of myself to guys from my cell phone. They say it's harmless fun. What should I do?"

Sonja N. Williams
Serial Tech Entrepreneur, Creator of Shock Theory-Interactive Marketing & Web Development and Urlyfe.com

A: "Don't do it! Who knows … you may become President one day, or a prestigious doctor, lawyer or even a minister. What you put in the Internet's public domain is just that—public. And it will stay there waiting for you to become the great princess that you are and it will resurface one day. Having fun as it relates to texting, the Internet and/or sending anything digitally to anyone is also about being responsible. You lose control over any and everything that leaves any gadget or computer that you consider fun. Stay safe by not sharing personal information and private photos of yourself. If not for anything else, then do it for the person you will become in the future."

* Jo Ann, 17

Q: "Is it safe for me to meet online friends off the Internet?"

Sonja N. Williams also offers this advice:

A: "Oftentimes we forget (Friends Without Faces) are still strangers. Many times people build emotional connections with people they meet on the Internet and become extremely comfortable—keep in mind predators understand this, and they are very patiently waiting for you to let your guard down. And while meeting people from the Internet offline has become popular, it is still a matter of using common sense. Depending on your age, I wouldn't encourage it. However, if you feel comfortable with doing so ALWAYS, ALWAYS meet in a public place—in the open, such as a mall during the day. Do not go to the movies, or be in enclosed areas regardless of how comfortable you are with the person. If possible, take someone with you, and the both of you remain in open, plain sight out in public."

CHECK IT OUT

X-block is designed for teens to not only promote Internet safety, but also encourages teens to become mentors ~ **www.xblock.isafe.org**

I-Safe is a website geared toward educating users about Internet safety ~ **www.isafe.org**

Wired Safety provides information and resources for victims of cyber stalking, cyber bullying, and cyber abuse ~ **www.wiredsafety.org**

NetSmartz Workshop, an interactive, educational safety resource to teach children and teens how to stay safer on the Internet, is a program of the National Center for Missing & Exploited Children ~ **www.netsmartz.org**

CHAPTER 9

Street Smartz

"No woman or girl anywhere in the world
should have to walk in fear or
live under the threat of violence."

—Hillary Clinton
U.S. Secretary of State

Think Quick! What would you do in this situation?

You're walking down a lonely street. A car slows down. The man driving starts to talk to you. What do you do?

A. Get closer to the car to see what he wants.

B. Ignore him, keep walking and minding your own business.

C. Start screaming and running in the opposite direction.

McGruff the Crime Dog from the National Crime Prevention Council advises:

> "Know what to do. Think No, Go, Yell, Tell. If you're in a dangerous situation, say no, run away, yell as loud as you can, and tell an adult."

My mom always taught me to make a scene to draw attention to myself. Attackers don't like a scene. And if I acted crazy, she said they would probably leave me alone.

Nowadays, things are different and more dangerous. It used to be that young folks had to be in before the streetlights came on. That was the rule. Try getting teens to do that in this day and age? Forget about it.

Today, you girls are more independent than ever. And in some ways, you're savvier than the teens in your mom's generation. The cool thing about that? It gives us extra time to spend with our friends. And a little bit more freedom ain't a bad thing, is it?

So you're out in the street. And your parents aren't around. You may find yourself in different situations and new places. All that smart decision-making is now in your hands. Of course, you want to go ahead and have yourself a good time.

This is the real world, though. And things happen. If you're not careful, your fun can turn into danger in a snap. You know a DivaGirl can't go out like that. We have to protect our future trailblazers, OK. So keep your eyes open and stay on your toes. And it's like the old folks used to say, "Keep your fist balled up in case something jumps off."

LEAVE A NOTE!

We know how it is sometimes. You might like doing things on the QT. And that's fine. After all, privacy is one of our constitutional rights. Sometimes we don't want people all up in our business, do we? But our safety comes first, BabyGirl. So going off the radar is not a good move. Hey, it can be downright crazy out there.

Think about leaving a paper trail. It's never a bad idea to let somebody know where you're going. So leave a note for your parents. Maybe you can tell a good friend your whereabouts. You never know. You could have an accident or get into who-knows-what kind of trouble.

Somebody you know and trust should know this information at all times:

- Where you'll be

- Who you're meeting

- When you plan to come back

They may need to contact you. Or you may need to contact them. Like we said, you never know …

Catch The Vibe

Listen carefully, Girls. Sometimes it's that little voice inside with a warning. It may be whispering, "Something's about to go down." Have you felt that way before? Sometimes it's in the pit of your stomach. It's a feeling you get when you realize that something's not right.

Maybe a person is giving off a bad vibe. Or things start to get a little shady. Are there other people around who can help you? Is there a way for you to get to safety? You should always be thinking about an exit plan. Learn to trust your instincts. If something in your gut says danger, it very well may be the case.

Sexual Assault Stats

- Someone in the United States is sexually assaulted every two minutes.

—U.S. Department of Justice's National Crime Victimization Survey

- About 73% of sexual assaults are committed by someone known to the victim.

—Rape, Abuse and Incest National Network

DATE SAFE

You've met someone who's fine, fun, and he's digging you. You're excited, yes? Are you that girl who calls your girlfriends so you can plot the next move? Whatever happens next, we want to make sure everything goes smoothly and safely.

Get to Know Him First: Sometimes our new guy is a total stranger. We need to get to know him before we get too comfortable.

Meet Your Internet Date: So you want to meet your virtual date in the real world. Do it in a public place. Quiz him to see if he's the same guy he claimed to be online. We need to check him out up close before we share any personal contact info.

Trial Run Before a First Date: See how he gets along with your friends. Invite him to hang in a group setting first. If you want to keep it cozy, try a double date. You can see how well he plays with others. And your friends can give him the OK.

Get out of the House: It's always best to meet in public rather than hanging out at home. You can meet at a restaurant, coffee shop, or the mall. On a first date, it can be way more fun to explore a place together.

Know Your Limitations: Be upfront with your date. If you have to, run down your checklist of don'ts. Let him know what your limits are from Jump Street. And you can tell your date the things you like to do as well. And you can ask your date what his limits are, too.

Set Some Ground Rules: OK, you're feeling the new guy. What now? If you want to spend time alone, that's natural. This is the time to establish some boundaries. Maybe it's still too soon for strolls through empty parks at night for you. What if you are in a parked car and things heat up? It's your prerogative if you want to cool things off.

Just Say No: You always have a right to say no. You always have a right to change your mind. If you're not comfortable with the way things are going, say "No!" with confidence. If he likes you, he will back off. If he starts to clown, get an exit strategy. He may respect you for standing your ground and ask you out again. If he doesn't, forget him for real.

Cut the Evening Short: Sometimes guys don't know how to act. So you may have to end your date sooner than you planned. You can play it smooth: "I have to get home. My parents are expecting me." If you feel threatened, find another way to get home. Call your parents or call a friend to come get you if there's no public transportation.

MAD MONEY

On a date, stash some cash. This is what we call mad money. They used to say if you got mad on a date, this was the money you used to get home. It used to be a quarter to use the pay phone. Now we have cell phones—so make sure they're charged. And a $20 bill should cover the taxi.

If you're stuck, try to contact the cops. Or go to any open business and ask the employees there to help you.

ALCOHOL + DRUGS = DANGER

Staying away from alcohol increases your chances of staying safe. If you engage in alcohol or drugs, you might run into trouble you may not be able to handle. It also makes it more of a challenge to escape dangerous situations.

You see what alcohol does to drivers who've been in accidents, right? Think about how it will affect your judgment. You may do things you normally wouldn't do with your safety.

Be careful if you're with someone who's been drinking or doing drugs. Those substances can make a person lose their mind. And that can be disastrous. Even a slight buzz can change your personality. Wouldn't you want your date to know the real you instead of the scuzzy-drunk you? And vice versa.

Drinks have also been used as a way to hurt women and teens. Date-rape drugs, like Ruffies, are slipped into drinks when people aren't looking. Did you know this is a common weapon used in sexual assaults? Drugging someone is a straight-up crime. Forcing someone who's not mentally or physically able to agree to sex is rape.

So BabyGirl, always get your own drink and open it yourself. That way, you'll know exactly what you're sipping. Keep your drink in your hands and don't leave it unattended. If you do put your drink down and walk away, just go and get yourself another one. Leave the first one on the table or pour it out.

Street Wise

When it comes to protecting yourself, prevention is the best defense. It pays off to pay attention to signs and signals. Sometimes we can decrease our chances of being in harm's way.

Attackers are always looking for easy targets. Now don't make it easy for them by falling asleep on a bus. On late nights, try to sit in front near the bus driver.

We've got to watch our body language, too. Looking lost can draw unwanted attention. A DivaGirl shows a sense of confidence, even if she's a little unsure. We should put some pep in our step and look like we know where we're going.

Take a look around when you get to a new place. Strange surroundings can sometimes be dangerous places. Do you feel safe in the place? Ask yourself: "Am I comfortable?"

Now size up your hangout buddies. Do they seem cool or shady? Is their behavior reckless or careful? If you're not feeling their vibe, that may be your cue to bounce.

Let's take some notes from the National Crime Prevention Council and other criminal justice experts:

- Walk in areas that are open, well lit, and well-traveled.

- Watch places where someone could hide like stairways and bushes.

- Avoid shortcuts that take you through isolated areas.

- Travel in a group if you're out late at night.

We don't have to be antsy every time we dot the door. But have some healthy fear and stay alert.

Your safety is usually in your own hands. You can stay safe and still have fun.

THE HANG OUT CHECKLIST

This is a checklist of things a girl should think about the minute she finds out she has some place to go:

How well do I know the crowd?

_____

_____

Is there someone there I can depend on?

_____

_____

What are people going to be doing?

_____

_____

Will there be alcohol or drugs?

_____

_____

Who knows where I'll be?

_____

_____

How will I get home?

_____

_____

Situations Where You're Most Vulnerable:

- Where drugs and alcohol are present

- A booty-call

- Hopping in somebody's car

- Being the only girl on the scene

IF IT HAPPENS TO YOU

If you've been sexually assaulted, try to break free from your attacker. Find a safe place and call for help. Go to a police station or hospital so they can assist you. It's a good idea if a friend can be there with you for emotional support.

The authorities will need to gather all the evidence from your attack. If you're still at the scene of the crime, don't touch anything. A medical professional or police should collect evidence. After that, it's OK to bathe, wash your hands, or brush your teeth. But make sure you've been examined first.

Though you may not have physical bruises, you're still at risk of getting an STD or having an unwanted pregnancy. Ask the health-care professional to conduct a Sexual Assault Forensic Exam (SAFE). If you think you've been drugged, ask the nurse to get a urine sample for evidence.

Write down all the details you can recall about the attack and the perpetrator.

Consider Counseling

Some physical wounds will heal faster than emotional or mental wounds. And those are the wounds we can't see? And you know what? They can be just as painful. An attack can leave us feeling scared and traumatized.

Counseling can help you deal with these difficult emotions. You can talk to a counselor privately. You can even get help over the phone. Or you can go to group sessions with people who've survived a similar experience.

Healing can be a process. So give yourself time to deal with what's happened. Just know you're not alone. And it's never too late to get help.

WHERE ELSE CAN I GO FOR HELP?

You can start with the National Sexual Assault Hotline **1-800-656-HOPE (4673)**. This confidential 24-7 hotline will connect you to your local crisis center. A counselor can explain the reporting process. They can tell you where to go and what to do. They may be able to send someone to accompany you.

If you're in a violent relationship, it can be a difficult subject to discuss. Know that violence against women is not OK. It doesn't matter if it's from a boyfriend or a stranger. If you're being abused, contact the National Domestic Violence Hotline **1-800-799-SAFE (7233)** or **1-800-787-3224 (TTY)** or check out **www.thehotline.org**.

Help is out there for us. That's the good thing. We have places to go and call, no matter where you live. You can get information on shelters, counseling, and legal aid. They can also answer your questions. Helpful organizations are ready to assist you if you ever need them. Check out **www.womens health.gov/violence-against-women/**

JUST LIKE YOU

* Dionna, 16

Q: "If I have a criminal record, will I be able to get a job or get into college? How long will I have to pay for my mistakes?"

Jeri Williams
**Chief of Police, Oxnard Police Dept.,
Ventura County, California**

A: "This is a tough question to answer without more facts. Some felonies committed will remain on your record forever. Some misdemeanors can be removed once you have completed probation/community service.

We all make mistakes. It's what you do after making the mistake that matters most times. Don't lie on an application. If you have done something, own the mistake, and advise the employer, school, etc. what happened and what you have done to keep from making the same mistake again.

Some experimental drug use may keep you from getting a job. You would have to check with the employer to determine what/how many times/how long ago the use of the drug has been to decide if they will accept you as a candidate."

* Rhett, 14

Q: "I live in a rough neighborhood. Do you have any advice on staying safe?"

Police Chief Jeri Williams offers these suggestions to Rhett:

A: "Pay attention to your surroundings! Know with whom you are hanging out. Tell others where and with whom you are going to be. Walk with confidence. Suspects are less likely to attack someone who looks confident.

If you get that funny feeling in your stomach telling you that the place you are or the person you are with is not a good place or good person, leave the area! We have been blessed with the gift of fear. We have to understand that when we think something may be wrong, most times it is!

Get to know the people in your neighborhood. That way, if someone you're not used to seeing around is there, you can call police.

Don't run/walk/exercise at night. If you do, don't go alone. You are asking for trouble."

CHAPTER 10

Rock Ya Body

"I've learned to love my body whether
I'm seven pounds heavier or seven pounds lighter.
I'm accepting of my body."

—Eva Mendes, Actress
Cosmopolitan

Who's that beautiful girl staring back at you in the mirror? Darling, it's you! Well, truth be told, many of us have our bad days: We may doubt our own beauty. And just a little reminder could do the trick. So there's no shame if that reminder has to come from us. We might have to break out that mirror and holla, "Girl, you look fab-u-lous!"

The movies and the magazines may not always see it that way. It seems like the media can have a jacked-up definition of beauty. Sometimes we don't see our reflections at all. And that's on them—because a DivaGirl is not to be dismissed. Got it?

Supermodel **Alek Wek** has the shortest hair, the fullest lips, and the darkest skin of any model on the scene today. Yet the catwalks in all the fashion capitals can't get enough of her alluring beauty. **Jennifer Lopez** has been celebrated for being bootylicious. And to think just a few years ago, big butts weren't always in style? Now plump rumps are the it-accessory of Hollywood.

Look, beauty should be about confidence, not anxiety. Has anyone ever told you that being beautiful means being a perfect size 6? Please, that's a flat-out lie. There's no such thing as perfection. If there were an image of a perfect girl, it would probably scare us. We might not realize it, but some people are amazingly beautiful because they're different from everybody else.

Sure, many of us indulge in that gazillion calorie Big Mac once in a blue moon. That burger can be hard to resist, so go ahead and enjoy it. Just be sure to enjoy some carrot sticks and spinach leaves for the rest of the day. And wash that down with some wheat grass juice. That will be all you can afford to eat in the calorie department after your Big Mac attack.

It's not all about counting carbs and calories. It's about doing you and being you! I know that we're all different, in a special way. So ask yourself what matters most …

- How do I keep in shape?
- What do I feed my body?
- How do I treat myself?

It all comes down to loving the skin you're in.

LOOK BOOK

Here's an activity to help you take a closer look at your body and the package you were given at birth. Take a photo of yourself in shorts and a fitted tank. You need to see the outline of your body. Supplies you'll need: pen, photo, tape, and journal.

Tape the photos in the journal. And jot down some thoughts about your physical features:

- Which physical feature gets you the most compliments?

- What makes you look different from other people?

- What physical feature makes people tease you?

_____

_____

- What makes you feel pretty?

_____

_____

- Now think about some things you may not like about your body.

_____

_____

- Are they things you can change?

_____

_____

- If not, can you accept them?

_____

_____

Try flipping what you think is a negative into a positive. For example, if you're teased for being dark skin, think about this. "People are paying big bucks on tanning to have dark skin." Kids sometimes teased girls, calling them "the young and the breastless." But at least they can fit into all the really cute tops.

_____

_____

_____

_____

_____

EVERYBODY'S GOT ISSUES

Beyoncé often talks about the struggles of squeezing into designer gowns when she was starting out in Destiny's Child. Now she has clothes custom made for her shape. **America Ferrera** was not your traditional sexy Latina, but that didn't keep her from starring in a groundbreaking prime-time comedy that went on to be a hit. And Miss America landed a recurring role on another hit prime time show, *The Good Wife*.

Consider these celebrities and their body images. **Queen Latifah** is a proud plus-size woman, but we often hear about her keeping her health in check through Jenny Craig or working out with a trainer. Another Jenny Craig success story is **Jennifer Hudson**. The Oscar winner lost more than 80 pounds on the weight-management program.

Dancer **Karina Smirnoff** is already in shape, but her chiseled body is evident that she has a fierce workout routine. And **Heidi Klum**, at 40-plus, can still rip the runway. How does she keep a banging body? She takes her exercising seriously.

This Is It

You gave yourself a once over. So are you down with making some positive changes in your routine? OK, let's get pumped up.

Now is this you? You can't stand sweating out your hair. It's foul when you have to rock a busted hairdo, especially in front of all the cute dudes. So you may not be trying to work up a sweat.

And what about losing those girlish curves? Some of you may not be ready to say goodbye to your extra junk. But exercise keeps everything tight and right. It tones the body, too. So don't fret about getting a smaller butt. Which is better: being toned or being unable to run across the street without getting out of breath?

You have to remember, your body is still developing as a young woman. So let's make some healthy decisions now, so you'll be fly at age 30.

What's so dope is you actually have the power to mold your body right now. On the upside, that's one of the benefits of exercising at this age. So if you don't want that round butt to turn to jiggling jelly, start running or at least walking three days a week.

MOVE IT

Truth is, there are a million things you'd probably rather be doing instead of hitting the gym. So we can always find excuses not to exercise.

Sometimes you need a motivator, a little sisterly kick in the butt. Is it a song that can get you on your feet? Do you have a good girlfriend or relative who can sweat along beside you? Do you need a cheering gallery to chant, "No pain, no gain?"

And we don't want you to overdo it on the treadmill until you pass out on the floor. Just take a peek at the bigger picture. Please realize that this picture goes beyond fitting into a pair of tight jeans or trimming down for the prom. We're talking little things you can do right now to make a change.

This is the best time to start good exercise habits at your age. I can testify that these habits will follow you for the rest of your life. (Consult with your physician before engaging in any strenuous exercise or diet plan.)

For real, exercise keeps you young, fit, and fabulous, which is probably not something stressing you now. But if you want to be 47 looking 27, you should stay physically active.

Working out can help you drop pounds, but it does so much more. It can be a wonder drug. The best thing about exercise is you don't need any health insurance: It's free. And if you to take this fitness drug regularly, you can prevent so many diseases. Nutrition experts say exercise helps to decrease high blood pressure, diabetes, heart disease, and obesity. And if you're black or Latino, those ailments affect your communities at higher rates. Exercise might even save you big on medical and hospital bills later.

I'm not saying you have to make huge commitments like working out for two hours, five days a week. Be honest with yourself and your body. If you've been inactive for years, you can't run a marathon after only two weeks of training. One thing is for sure, healthy bodies rule!

EAT FOR BEAUTY

You may have heard the phrase: Eat for Life. But the phrase should be Eat for Beauty because she's certain that a good diet is part of her inner beauty arsenal. A girl who eats well puts forth her best skin possible.

Fit Bit #1

Take it from the queen of the hip-hop workout.
Former Miss Fitness International **MaDonna Grimes**
has 5 simple steps you can't beat:

1. Try signing up for one movement activity a
    year. For instance, try soccer, baseball, cheer-
    leading, marching band, track, football,
    musical theater, or roller-blading.

2. McDonald's is not totally bad. Stay away from the
    sandwiches. Try the Southwestern Grilled Chicken
    Salad with the Balsamic Vinaigrette.

3. Before school, when you wake up, wake up
    your body. Stretch and do abs for 5 minutes
    on the living-room floor or in your bedroom
    before washing your face.

4. And 20 minutes of Cardio is your lifesaver. I
    mean any continuous movement—walking,
    jump-roping, swimming, dancing, etc.—will keep
    your weight at a healthy good-looking level.

5. Try to eat with friends or family. If someone
    speaks to you while you're eating, you tend to
    eat slower and get fuller faster. Eat until your
    body is satisfied, and not until you feel too full.

Fɪᴛ Bɪᴛ #2

If you're feeling up for it, soccer legend
Eddie Pope *has a challenge for you. The Major*
League All-Star and National Soccer Hall of Famer
wants you to kick it up a notch. He designed a
5-step program just for you:

1. **Get at Least 60 Minutes of Exercise a Day.** Try
   to move for 60 continuous minutes. It can be
   one activity or a combination.
   a. Mix it up during the day with 20 minutes of
      jump-roping, 30 minutes of Zumba, and 10
      minutes of dancing.
   b. Take a 60-minute class (like a hip-hop
      dance class).
   c. Participate on a sports team, and during
      the off days or practice days, run or do
      some other physical activity.

2. **Stretch Before and After Exercising.** In order
   to make sure you're getting the most out of
   your workout, your muscles need to be nur-
   tured. That means getting them ready by
   stretching them out before an activity and
   cooling them down once you are finished.
   They need to recover and repair.

3. **Eat Well. Eat to Live; Don't Live to Eat.** The majority of your daily diet should be fruits, vegetables, and whole grains. You should try to include a portion of lean proteins and limit the amount of fats you eat in a day. Good sources of protein include chicken, turkey, fish, egg whites. Good fats include things like nuts and certain fish.

   Try to keep sweets to a minimum, but never deprive yourself. Eating the proper portions makes a difference. The next time you eat, ask yourself, "Is what I'm choosing to eat a good choice or is there a better one?" You will begin to change the way you think about food and soon you will automatically be making good choices.

4. **Stay Hydrated! Drink Plenty of Water, Especially When Exercising.** Your body needs to have water to operate properly and help fight certain ailments (like urinary tract infections). You should have at least 64 ounces of water per day, and shoot for 88 to 96 ounces when exercising.

   An easy way to make sure you get the recommended amount is to use one or two water bottles that hold at least 20 to 24 ounces of

water. Keep the bottle(s) with you, continuously refilling them throughout the day with the last bottle being consumed in the evening prior to going to bed.

By purchasing a reusable water bottle (Wal-Mart or Target), you will save money by not purchasing bottled water and help the environment by reducing, recycling, and reusing.

5. **Get a Good Night's Sleep.** Be sure to get 8 hours of sleep a night. You should try to be in bed by 10 p.m., 11 p.m. at the latest. Your body needs adequate rest in order for tips 1, 2, 3, and 4 to have the optimal effect on your health and help strengthen your mind. This gives it time to recover, repair, and prepare for the next day.

These tips are designed to help you be good to yourself. There's just one you! Your future can be great but you have to be able to make it happen—physically, emotionally, mentally, and spiritually. If you follow these five tips, you will be making choices to strengthen your body and your mind.

GREAT FACE 101

Millie Bell, President of DermHA & Skin Health Solutions, is a skin care guru. This former model-turned-licensed medical esthetician has some healthy diet tips every girl ought to know:

- Drink at least eight glasses of water a day to keep the body functioning properly. Too little can cause dizziness, headaches, constipation, and dark circles under the eyes.

- Eat a high-fiber diet. This is important for keeping the colon clean and ridding the body of toxins.

- Eat lots of fruit. This is always good for the skin because of the nutritional value and water content of fruit.

- Try eliminating dairy products from your diet for one month. Acne may develop due to an allergic reaction to dairy products.

- Try to avoid all forms of sugar since it can become addictive. Sugar feeds cancer cells and contributes to heart disease, diabetes, acne, and premature aging.

Healthy Girls Rock!

Seems like everybody is talking about living a healthy lifestyle.

First Lady **Michelle Obama** is championing the cause with her "Let's Move" campaign to raise healthier kids. She is not playing when it comes to winning the battle of the bulge. Join her fitness challenge at **www.letsmove.gov**.

Beyoncé teamed up with the First Lady for the "Let's Move" campaign to promote physical education at local schools with her *Move Your Body* flash workout video. Check out the army of students working out with her on youtube.com. You can download the full instructional video at the National Association of Broadcasters Education Foundation's website at **www.nabef.org**.

The USDA's new Food Guide Pyramid can help you plan nutritious meals and snacks. The website has a free online tool called MyPyramid Menu Planner. Enter information about your daily habits to check if your diet is balanced. Visit **www.mypyramidtracker.gov/planner/launchPage.aspx**.

And smart snacking could be the key. It can hold you over until your next meal. You know how it is when your tummy starts growling. Some of us reach for a Snickers or head to the golden arches. But throwing some healthy snacks in our bag may keep us on the right track.

Check out some delicious food swaps at **www.hungrygirl.com**. There, Hungry Girl has the scoop on the healthiest snacks like ice cream, chips, and cookies. But when it comes to those cravings for barbecued ribs and frosted cupcakes, you sometimes have to strum up the will power to just say NO!

FOOD JOURNAL

Write down your typical meals. Keep it real. Write down how many and fruit and vegetable servings you have each day.

What are your favorite fruits?

_____

_____

_____

What are your favorite veggies?

_____

_____

_____

Here's The Skinny On Eating Out

If you're a girl on the go, some days eating out may be your only option. Restaurants and fast-food chains don't have to be the enemy; we can still think fit. Here are some simple reminders and smart food swaps from the USDA.

- Ask for water or order fat-free or low-fat milk, unsweetened tea, or drinks without added sugars.

- Opt for whole-wheat bread for sandwiches.

- Start your meal with a salad packed with veggies, to help control hunger and feel satisfied sooner.

- Get the salad dressing on the side, then use only as much as you want.

- Select main dishes that include vegetables, such as stir fries, kebobs, or pasta with a tomato sauce.

- Order steamed, grilled, or broiled dishes instead of those that are fried or sautéed.

- Choose a small or medium portion; this includes main dishes, side dishes, and beverages.

- Skip the "all-you-can-eat" buffet; or order an item from the menu instead.

- Pick foods that do not have creamy sauces or gravies.

- Add little or no butter to your food.

- Choose fruits for dessert most often.

If main portions at a restaurant are larger than you want, try one of these strategies to keep from overeating:

- Order an appetizer-sized portion or a side dish instead of an entrée.

- Share a main dish with a friend.

- If you can chill the extra food right away, take leftovers home in a doggy bag.

- When your food is delivered, set aside or pack half of it to go immediately.

- Resign from the Clean Your Plate Club; when you've eaten enough, leave the rest.

- On long commutes or shopping trips, pack some fresh fruit, cut-up vegetables, low-fat string cheese sticks, or a handful of unsalted nuts to help you avoid stopping for sweet or fatty snacks.

—U. S. Department of Agriculture
~www.choosemyplate.gov/healthy-eating-tips/tips-for-eating-out.html

HEALTHY HINT

Remember what your grandma used to say: Start your morning out right. Breakfast is the most important meal of the day. Don't miss it!

Your Space

Let's get it started!

Write down some everyday activities that will get your body moving.

Ex. Walking instead of riding the bus

Ex. Doing leg lifts while chatting on the phone

_____

_____

_____

Let's turn up the heat!

Write down some other physical activities you can enjoy.

Ex. Riding my bike across town

Ex. Taking a dance class at the community center

_____

_____

_____

Let's take our time!

Write down some ways to make room in your schedule to exercise.

Ex. Cut my Internet time in half

Ex. Include my friends in my workout plans

_____

_____

_____

Let's get fit!

Write down your fitness goals for the next month.

Ex. I want to exercise at least four days a week

Ex. I will walk to school everyday for a month

_____

_____

_____

DANGEROUS DIETS

Experts say these are some of the dangers of dieting:

1. Most diets don't give you all the nutrients you need to eat healthy every day. They restrict certain foods that are important for a balanced diet.

2. You'll become a yo-yo dieter, which means your weight will go up and down. You lose the weight, and then you'll gain it back. This can cause depression, heart disease, and diabetes.

3. It starts with normal diets. But usually the dieter becomes obsessed with weight loss. It can have harmful effects on your menstrual cycle and organ functions. It could also lead to deadly results.

- **ANOREXIA NERVOSA** Starving yourself or over-exercising to burn more calories.

- **BULIMIA** Over-eating and forcing yourself to vomit or using laxatives to aid in bowel movements.

> "In the United States, as many as 10 million females and 1 million males are fighting a life and death battle with an eating disorder such as anorexia or bulimia."
>
> —The National Eating Disorder Association

For additional information on eating disorders, go to **www.nationaleatingdisorders.org**

Just Like You

* Sherron, 18

Q: "I'm a great singer, but I don't look like Beyoncé and some of the other stars. It seems like success is as much about looks as it is about talent. I've got the skills, but can I make it if I'm not a size 4?"

The Late Mia Amber Davis
Plus-Size Model, Actress, and TV Producer

A: "Society has changed so much in the past few years or so due to the surge of reality TV and the advancements of technology, social media, and the like. As a result, we have become a nation obsessed with celebrity, and we have gained a strong sense of entitlement, while developing a demand for instant gratification. True talent seems to no longer be the pathway to fame. Time and time again we have watched as someone who 'looks the part,' but may not have the vocal, acting or any ability to entertain, shoots to stardom seemingly overnight.

At the same time, it's amazing to bare witness as the fashion industry opens its arms to a curvier silhouette although my industry, plus-size modeling, now begins at a size 6. Yes, women 5'10 and size 6 are representing the 62% of the women in this country who wear a size 14 and higher.

The music industry has always been influenced by the fashion industry and vice versa. While fuller frames are slowly being introduced into the mainstream fashion industry (by plus models such as Crystal Renn), there have only been a handful of curvy performers (like Wynona Judd) to take the music world by storm.

Since the golden age of Hollywood when 'flippers' or plastic teeth were added to the cherubic smiles of young stars like Shirley Temple to make them 'perfect,' or as superstar Janet Jackson just revealed, her breasts were bound to make her appear younger and more streamlined as she played Penny on *Good Times*, or as anyone who has watched the TLC network megahit *Toddlers and Tiaras* and seen a 5-year-old getting her eyebrows waxed … looks count!

It's horrible but true in entertainment. Skills, talent, and ability should be at the forefront, but they seem to be seen as a bonus, not as a prerequisite.

Look back to the 1980s when music veteran and full-figured singer Martha Wash was replaced by a straight-sized model who lip-synched to Martha's voice in music videos because of Martha's size. Look at the incredible vocals of Jill Scott or Jazmine Sullivan who are not shaped like Beyoncé and therefore may not have as great a commercial success as she has had. But there's only one Beyoncé, and there's only one YOU!

Do I believe you must be a certain size to make it in this industry? Yes and no. I still believe in the power of true talent above all else, but I also know that if you don't look a certain way, the industry will not look

twice in your direction. Performers like Beyoncé and the unconventional Lady Gaga have trained and prepared literally all their lives for the opportunities they are being blessed with right now. They study and give the industry no reason and no room to say no to them or their abilities.

If you are talented, are strong in your convictions, love and nurture your talents, are a well-versed student of your industry, and are prepared to keep pushing no matter what opposition may come your way because you do not fit the physical mold set for celebrity, then you will make it no matter what your size.

I, for one, don't believe in 'no!' In no way do I fit the mold of a traditional plus-size model or actress, but I am studying every day and finding new ways to get myself out there to spread my message of self-acceptance and shatter societal beauty ideals.

You've got to keep pushing, keep praying, keep studying and keep believing that you have something special to share with the world. You've got to be ready to share your talents with any and everyone who will listen to you at any given moment. It may seem unfair, but you may have to sing a little harder and shine a little brighter to make them see through your curves and focus on your talents. But as soon as you

open your mouth, they will undoubtedly know that Curvy Girls Rock.

I believe in you, but more importantly, you should believe in you. Now … Go be great!"

CHECK IT OUT

Take steps to a healthier you at the USDA's website designed to encourage you take control of your diet ~ **www.mypyramid.gov**

Young Women's Health offers girl-friendly information about teen health, diet, fitness and sexuality ~ **www.youngwomenshealth.org**

Hungry Girl is a fun and fantastic blog that gives delicious healthy alternatives to our favorite fatty foods ~ **www.hungry-girl.com**

Dove Campaign for Real Beauty empowers and arms girls with important facts and information teens will appreciate ~ **www.dove.us**

MaDonna Grimes' 3-in-1 DVD showcases the queen of hip-hop fitness dance as she brings you a 90-minute collection of routines for a cardio-sculpt workout and teaches you step-by-step how to dance ~ **www.madonnagrimes.com**

CHAPTER 11

Be a Cover Girl

"I'm not ugly, but my beauty is a total creation."

—Tyra Banks
Fashion Mogul

I was destined to be a cosmetic mogul. I was going to launch a successful skin care line. It's all I could think about as a teen. And I would go down in history for finding the fountain of youth and putting it in a bottle.

I was obsessed with having healthy skin. I would read everything I could about products that promised to work miracles. I questioned if they really worked.

Today, there are all kinds of information and products available for every skin tone under the sun. And it's just a click away. It's not always about the hype, either. Many items you see on TV or with a celebrity endorsement may not always be the best brand for your skin. Take the challenge to read up on skin health and other beauty-related stuff. There's nothing better than an educated consumer. She's the best beauty customer.

Girl who knows, you might want to launch your own product line or chain of beauty boutiques. But you first have to learn what's good and what's right to maintain the health of the skin. If you like, go on and enhance it with touches of makeup.

For now, stay on track to do what you need to re-juvenate and maintain the great face you have. Do it now! Build that strong foundation. Because at the end of the day, it's about putting your best face forward.

BEAUTY SECRET #1

* LEAN, 14, WANTS TO KNOW...

Q: "What can I do now to maintain clean, clear,
      and healthy skin?"

Millie Bell
President, DermHA & Skin Health Solutions

A: "Clear, healthy skin starts from the inside out.
      Develop daily habits now so that they'll become
      second nature. Make healthy choices when it comes to
      eating. Fresh fruits and vegetables are always at the
      top of the list, and the more colorful they are, the
      healthier.

      Cut out fried foods, sodas, sugars, and processed
      foods as much as possible because they drain your
      body of nutrients. Drink 8 to 10 glasses of water a day
      and more if you do sports or exercise programs.
      Exercise daily and include walking whenever possible.

      During your teens, hormones create a variety of
      changes in your body and on your skin. To make sure
      it stays healthy, you have to keep it clean. In my
      opinion, cleansing your skin in the morning and at
      night is the most important step in a skin-care
      regimen.

Use a water-based moisturizer to keep skin hydrated, and choose skin-care products that are free of major irritants like fragrance, alcohol, lanolin, and dyes. If you have severe acne with cysts or infection, you should see a dermatologist to prevent scarring.

If you get a pimple, apply a dot of pure tea tree oil on pimples or pustules to kill the bad bacteria but not the good kind. Don't touch the affected areas unless your hands are clean. Don't squeeze the skin beneath!"

Fresh Faces

You want a fresh face? Use fresh makeup. The good news is most brands contain preservatives to keep out bacteria. The bad news is the preservatives get weaker over time. So old makeup can be a playground for bacteria.

For that reason, beauty experts suggest tossing aging makeup. How old is too old? Here's the lowdown on the shelf life of cosmetics.

- **Eye makeup** (shadows, mascara and liner): Three months

- **Foundation**: Nine months

- **Pressed powder compacts**: Four months

- **Lipstick**: Six months

If you're going to use makeup, get some tips on makeup safety at **www.girlshealth.gov/body/ grooming/makeup.cfm**

> ## COVER GIRL TIP
> Crank up the glam factor for special occasions, visit a cosmetic counter at a department store. Often times, makeup artists will give you a complimentary makeover. If you can, slip them a $5 or $10 tip. Sometimes you could just purchase one of their products as a courtesy.

BEAUTY SECRET #2

* SHONDA, 15, WANTS TO KNOW...

Q: "What are some simple makeup tips I can use for day and night looks without looking like a hooker?"

Celebrity Makeup Artist Anthony Jones
(Clients: Beyoncé, Mary J. Blige, Glamour)

A: "**Foundation:** Match your foundation with your neck color. Don't match it to your face and hands; that's not your true skin color. That way you won't have to worry about wearing foundation on your neck, which can ruin your clothes.

Cheeks: Go easy with the blush. You should start in the back and work your way to the front. Blow off the excess powder and gradually add color. It's supposed

to be blush: You don't want to look like you've been punched in the face.

Lips: Your lip liner should be the color of your lipstick or a shade darker. Don't wear brown lip liner unless that is the color of your lipstick.

Eyes: Skip the smoky eye. It's too dramatic for teens. Go for soft neutral shades on the eyes with hints of pink. In fact, you could go without shadow altogether.

Do a little eyeliner and just line the upper lid with a brown or black pencil depending on the complexion of your skin tone. And add a little brown or black mascara depending on your hair color.

Thick lashes on young girls can look ridiculous. If you're 17, individual lashes are fine, as long as they look natural. The glue can be harmful. So a lash strip would be better.

Brows: If you have thick brows, go for a slight arch. They should be groomed if they are wild. It's best to have them professionally done. Opt for a shave instead of waxing and tweezing, which can destroy the elasticity on your brow area and cause sagging over time.

Stay away from the white eye pencil. It should be applied professionally. It could make you look like a clown if you don't know what you're doing.

Take care of your skin. Wear a little lip gloss, mascara, a little lip liner, and eyeliner. And that will be enough."

THE BLEND TREND

Please check your neck. You see girls make this mistake all the time: We can see where their makeup stops and their neck begins. We don't want you going out like that. Remember to blend your foundation gradually as you get near the hairline and neck area.

MANE ATTRACTIONS

Remember this hair 'do: rock those locks! Here are some classic styles:

Be Blunt!

Wave It!

Super Curl!

Pony Up!

Illustrations by Waren K. Bradley

BEAUTY SECRET #3

* ANGELA, 16, WANTS TO KNOW...

Q: "My hair is dry and ridiculously curly. My relaxers barely last six weeks. How can I maintain my style?"

Celebrity Hair Stylist Karen Bishop
(Clients: Tyra Banks, Nia Long, Angela Bassett)

"Permanently relaxing your hair is a great way to soften and straighten hair that is super curly. Hence the word "perm." This terminology is used to describe what relaxers do to the bonds in our hair. It permanently changes the characteristic of the bonds inside the cuticles.

There are straightening perms and curly perms. When we speak of relaxers, we are speaking of straightening relaxers. Technically, the duration of relaxers is from four to six weeks. If you are having a problem with the duration of your relaxer, rejoice because that means your hair is healthy and grows effortlessly.

Combating dry hair is conquered by using moisture. The opposite of dry is wet, not oil. When shampooing, use moisturizing, or hydrating shampoos. When conditioning, use moisturizing, or specially formulated for dry hair conditioners. Steam conditioning is also a great way to deliver moisture to the hair."

BEAUTY SECRET #4

* FARRAH, 17, WANTS TO KNOW...

Q: "My hair is straight, limp and oily. How can I keep it healthy and give it body."

Karen Bishop has an answer for Farrah, too...

A: "Oily hair stems from over-active sebacious glands, which is internal. To combat oily hair, we must deal with it externally. There are oily scalp treatments on the market. Search for a deep cleansing and exfoliating treatment and gently massage your scalp. Look for J.F. Lazartigue, which has an excellent treatment for oily scalp, then use a deep cleansing shampoo. This will open the pores in the scalp and allow the oil to come out to be neutralized and cleansed. This also regulates the sebum. Follow up with an intensive sebum treatment. This will help restore the balance of oily scalp, leaving hair healthy with body."

FIND YOUR LOOK

Here some questions to ask yourself to help find the best hairdo that suits you:

1. What's my personality type? Ex. free spirit, laid back, conservative.

_____

_____

2. What type of career do I have? Full-time student, athlete, summer intern, part-timer?

_____

_____

3. What kind of hairstyle is for me? Relaxed, curly, natural, cropped, shoulder-length, extensions?

_____

_____

4. What's my beauty budget? I can spend $ _____ per week or month on my hair.

5. What is the shape of my face? Oval, round, triangle, inverted triangle, diamond, square?

_____

_____

6. Do I want a high- or low-maintenance hairstyle? I do/don't have much time to spend on my hair.

_____

_____

BEAUTY SECRET #5

* MING LEE, 16, WANTS TO KNOW...

Q.   "I like to get punked out with crazy colors in my hair every week. But my hair has been coming out in plugs. What can I do to rock some fun colors without going bald?"

Celebrity Hair Stylist Kimmi Hendrix
(Clients: Disney, Ashley Tisdale, Celebrity Aprentice)

A.   "I love when younger divas choose to express their individuality with fierce hairstyles and fashion! But I'm so sorry to hear about your hair loss. First order of business is treating your hair and scalp so you can stop further breakage and hair loss. You want to give your hair some TLC by applying a restorative protein treatment followed with big-time moisture. A great product to use is the Aphogee Two Step Protein Treatment, which typically comes with everything you need in one kit. You can find this in full and trial sizes at your local beauty supply store such as Sally's Beauty Supply (Tip: If you sign up for the Sally Beauty Club card you get sweet discounts!).

OK, so now that hair health is out of the way, I usually recommend that my younger clients stay away from permanent or semi-permanent colors because it causes so much stress on young tresses. Since

applying color correctly is super tricky, it's better to go for more temporary routes of expressing yourself.

Here are some options for you:

Temporary Hair Color: If you want bright, vibrant colors, try the Manic Panic DyeHard® Temporary Color Styling Gel. This product is a thick temporary gel color that comes in a squeezable tube and is easy to apply. They have tons of colors and can be used on all hair textures. This product is also a moderate holding gel as well, but the key is that the color coverage is great and even better can be washed out when you're done! No damage, no commitment, no worries.

Clip-on Hair Pieces: When you want just a splash of color without the time commitment, clip-on hair pieces are perfect. They come in a ton of different colors as well as patterns, like zebra print! Also, these pieces are available in synthetic and human hair versions and are made in various textures to match your own (or maybe if you're bold you can do a slightly different texture for dimension). The synthetic versions are less versatile because you can't apply heat or product, but they are less expensive. Human hair pieces are more flexible and can be styled similar to your own hair but they generally cost more. Either one looks fab if you place them strategically, so you can't go wrong.

Tinsel & Feather Hair Extensions: To try out some alternatives to color, you can incorporate tinsel and feather hair extensions. The tinsel comes in a few flashy colors and is easy to install by simply tying the colorful strand to your hair. They sparkle and shimmer so it's really amazing to see at night. Feathers are also an interesting way to add flair, but you'll need to go to a professional to install the extension because there's a special device and bead used to attach to your hair.

I hope you find these tips helpful and inspiring. It's awesome to push the envelope on style but hair health is the key. Make sure you get regular trims or haircuts, use gentle shampoos and conditioners, and avoid excessive heat. Last but not least, be the best you and stay amazing!"

NAIL FILES

These days, going to the nail salon is just as routine as going to the beauty shop. A neat manicure is just another way for us to feel pampered and look our best. But all kinds of dangers lurk when we visit the manicurist. We have to worry about germs and bacteria. We've got to be careful to protect the health of our nails.

Your nail salon should be spotlessly clean and state licensed (see if it's posted on the wall). Does your manicurist scrub the station and soaking tub between clients? This is something you can request. Who wants to stick her feet in an unsanitary tub?

Your manicurist should have clean hands with no cuts on the skin. A manicurist can also wear plastic gloves, as long as it's a new pair for each client. The tools should be sterilized by ultraviolet heat or the cold method. If you're not comfy with the salon's cleanliness, find a new manicurist.

MANI-PEDI TIPS

- Bring your own nail kit with clippers, files, and other instruments to avoid infections.

- Push back cuticles. Cutting them can cause bacteria, yeast infections, and hepatitis.

- Wait to shave your legs after a pedicure. Bacteria in the water could irritate them.

- Skip the nail filing before applying acrylics. It can take thin nails months or years to heal.

- Limit the time you wear acrylic nails. If you wear them for too long, bacteria and fungus will attack. And chemical adhesives can cause allergic reactions.

JUST LIKE YOU

* LAJEAN, 14

Q: "What makeup brands would you recommend for a
teen girl on a budget?"

Celebrity Makeup Artist Darya Latham
(Clients: Maxim, Naturi Naughton, Shape)

A: "Fortunately, there are many inexpensive and
fabulous makeup brands to choose from to fit
anyone's budget. I recommend brands like NYX. This
brand has a fabulous and vast variety of color for eye
shadows, lipsticks, lip liners, and eyeliners. The
products are highly pigmented, and the quality is
excellent!

If you are looking for a specific shade foundation and
powders to perfectly match darker complexions, I
highly recommend Black Opal cosmetics. Try Cover
Girl and NYC makeup for lighter or paler skin tones.
These products can be found at your local drugstores.
Another amazing and affordable line is NYC makeup,
which offers a variety of products. I'm fond of their
loose powders and their liquid eyeliners and lip
glosses.

If you're looking for a fabulous mascara, try Great
Lash by Maybelline. My personal new favorite
mascara is Colossal Lash because it gives lashes a

mega boost of volume and length. You're sure to make a lasting, cute impression with a single bat of your eyelashes with such a classic brand. The line is inexpensive but very effective."

* VALERIE, 13

Q: "How often should I have my weave washed and redone?"

CELEBRITY HAIR STYLIST WILLIAM ROBINSON
(Clients: Naomi Campbell, Lauryn Hill, Jill Scott)

A: "Try two months. It's vital that you remove your weave every eight weeks because your hair is alive. Just like a plant, your hair needs air to breathe. When your hair is braided for more than two months, the shedding that happens normally turns to smothering and breakage. Hair needs to be combed out and trimmed before you redo your weave. This will help maintain the health of your hair."

Your Space

What have you learned about yourself and your look in this chapter? It would be good to write it down so you don't forget when you're ready to get a fabulous new 'do.

CHAPTER 12

Ready for the Red Carpet

"The things I tell my girls are the things I would tell you:
'Do not be afraid to fail or be afraid to take risks in life.
Learn to use your voice now. Ask questions. Ask stupid questions.
Be laughed at. Get it wrong. Trip, fall and then get back up.'"

—Michelle Obama
First Lady of the United States

Life sure is funny. My high school guidance counselors wouldn't have known what to make of my
future. Suppose I had told them that I would've
done the exciting things I've done and been the
fabulous places I've been. And Girl, what if I told
them I strolled a few red carpets myself along the
way. They would've rolled on the floor, got up and
laughed right in my face.

I mean, my grades were a little horrific. I had been kicked out of school—and my mother's home. Many people told me I didn't stand a chance. But I knew something they didn't: I'm not to be counted out.

That's what I've taught the girls who walk through the doors of the Evoluer House. It never mattered to me how messed up their story was. Some people may think you're down for the count. But I know a person's past doesn't always dictate their future.

I've had girls who were labeled ugly ducklings go on to have international modeling careers. I've had big-mouth girls who worked everybody's last nerve go on to be successful attorneys at top law firms. I've had girls who were the daughters of drug dealers and addicts who went on to graduate from college and become respectable business leaders in corporate America.

That's what we call flipping it. That's when you turn your negative into a positive. You make the best of what you're given. Now some girls may have a similar situation. And they can't see their way through that long dark, foggy path. Many times they just give up. Then there are those girls who may not know what's at the end of the road. Yet they keep going and keep trying. And when the fog clears they come out a winner. That's the DivaGirl in her.

IT'S YOUR MOVE

Now, where do you go from here? It's time to strategize. Let's get a good game plan and figure out your next move. On second thought, make that your next moves with an "s." First you've got to set some goals.

You want to have an idea of what success could look like for you. Your goals should be clear and to the point. And HoneyGirl, please be honest with yourself; your goals do need to be realistic. Still though, aim for the stars. And don't be afraid to push up the sky.

This chart may be just the motivation you need. Post it to your wall or anyplace where you'll see it every day. Fill in your goals for the week. Check the box each day if you accomplished this task. Cut yourself some slack if you skip a day. Ready to go?

THINGS I NEED TO DO	S	M	T	W	T	F	S

Know Yourself?

By now, you've had a chance to give yourself the once-over, up and down. Maybe you know who you are. Or maybe, you're still figuring it out. Either way, it's all good. You have some ideas to help shape your opinion of yourself.

- You probably realized a list of things you enjoy doing. On that list, there has to be a few areas where you excel. Perhaps you've found a hidden talent you never knew you had. Or maybe you discovered your special gift.

- You have a role model who's putting it down in her field. You can use her résumé as a roadmap. Keep an eye on her. Watch her ups to see how she's succeeded and her downs to see how she's recovered.

- It's about taking something positive from your experiences. Along the way, you'll realize what your purpose is in the world. And SuperGirl, you'll be miles ahead of the pack.

Keep Up The Momentum

Write the goals you're working on here:

_____

_____

_____

You've set your goals. Here goes the tough part. Here's where we really have to psyche ourselves up to do things we may not normally do. We might have to make some changes in our regular routine if we want to meet our goals. Are you trying to improve your grades? Maybe you're looking for a new job. That could mean less time for chilling with friends. Say to yourself, "I don't care what they say. I don't care what they do. My eyes are on my future, and I can feel my change coming."

ON THE MONEY

Think you've got what it takes to go out there and handle your business? I think you do! You've been eyeing that job that fits your personality. You've found a way to put your talent and skills to good use. And really, this could help you gain more experience for what you want to do later down the road. I say, go for it.

- Practice with a friend. Have her run through a mock interview with you. Answer the questions as intelligently as you can. And don't forget, your body language is answering questions, too.

- So what you don't have a lengthy résumé. Babysitting can show that you work well with children. Ironing for the family could be great experience for a trendy boutique. Get creative and add those chores to your résumé.

- You've met our teen entrepreneurs. Do you think you can start your own business? Take a page from how those young ladies started a jewelry line, animal balloon-making company, and dance studio.

CLASS ACT

Being professional is a sign that you are growing up. It's never too early to step on that career ladder. Hey, the earlier you start, the higher you can climb. You've got to watch your step though: Everyone else is.

ACTING THE PART

Rules of etiquette and home training may sound a little old school. But there's nothing corny about it. You won't lose any cool points. You'll just be keeping it classy. And being sophisticated never goes out of style. It makes a big difference in what people make of you. So mind your Ps and Qs.

- At your next big shindig, work the crowd like it's your party. You'll be making small talk like you're a pro. Personal questions can be a turn-off. So try to keep the conversation light and general.

- Still don't know which fork to use? Work your way from the outside in, after each course is served.

And if you can play it off, BabyGirl, just watch what others are doing to see if it looks correct.

- Make sure your friends get the DivaGirl's memo on how to behave in certain social circles. Feel free to invite them to professional settings, just be careful about mixing business with playtime.

DECODING MESSAGES

Your body sends all kinds of messages. And people are watching and listening. You may say or do something, and it could come off the wrong way. Try to decode what your words and actions mean to other people.

- Your poise and posture will reveal a lot of clues about you. MissGirl, you've got to watch how you stand and how you sit. Be a natural at maintaining good eye contact and watch the fidgeting.

- We love colorful language. Let's just make sure it's all said in English, so we're well understood. Save the Pig Latin and Ebonics for chat time with your crew. Carry a little pocket thesaurus with you if you must.

- Talking trash about your friends behind their backs is not cute. And calling them out of their names can be a bad move. On second thought, calling her Brilliant or Beautiful kinda has a nice ring.

CHART YOUR PROGRESS

Give yourself a time frame and schedule some deadlines. This will help you track your progress. Check off the boxes on your to-do chart to measure your success. Review your efforts often to maintain motivation and momentum.

You can even post your goals and charts on the fridge, so your family can get in on the action. If someone is expecting you to do something, that might light a fire under you. Too much pressure? Maybe you'd feel more comfortable sharing your goals with your girlfriends. They might even have some suggestions that would be helpful to you.

TRICKS FOR SUCCESS

Keep your eyes on the prize. Is your plan to psych yourself into gear working? If not, you might need some new motivation tricks. It could be a lack of interest in your goal. It's cool if your goals change. Hey, that's your right. And it's your future.

Make a poster of you that shows the benefits of you reaching your goals. If singing is your thing, paste your mug shot on Mariah Carey's body. When you squint, you'll see yourself performing at Radio City Music Hall. You want to work for NASA? Download a photo of Astronaut Mae Jemison and post your picture next to hers.

Check Yourself

Sometimes, you need to proceed with caution. Keep your eyes open when you're out on your daily travels. Be safe when you venture off into cyberspace. And watch the traffic riding down lover's lane.

Work It Out

As any DivaGirl works the red carpet, she learns to embrace her beauty. If you don't think you're beautiful, who will? We may have had to redefine what is beautiful for ourselves. Some of us had to learn to love our thick thighs or bony legs. The point is, we are rocking what our mama gave us, curves and all. And yes, we like what we see staring us back in the mirror, thank you!

- Do it, Girl! But don't overdo it. We can start out with a little walk. Before you know, we might be able to jog. If a marathon is in your future, go for it. Just see what your doctor prescribes before lacing up your track shoes.

- Diets are for the birds. Healthy girls rock! Next time, try to skip that drive-through at Taco Bell. Pack a tuna on wheat with mustard to go. And keep an apple in your handbag. Your tummy might be glad you did.

- Everyone's not meant to be a size 2 or size 6. We're living healthy lifestyles today, so we can be fly and fit at 30. And by the time we're 40? Please, people will be mistaking us for a woman in her 20s.

BEING BEAUTIFUL

You know beauty comes in all shapes and colors. You can be made up with the perfect shades and hues of the season. Or you can be totally bare and au naturel. Either way, the glam squad and skincare experts have given you tips on serving up a great face.

- Keep things light when it comes to wearing makeup. You'll have plenty of time to pile on the goo when you're older and you're trying to look young again.

- A cleansing and moisturizing routine every day is an investment that will pay off with compliments later. And sunscreen can help keep your skin looking ageless.

- We've shared one beauty secret after another. But here's the best way to figure out what beauty is. It's not a big secret at all. Just look in the mirror.

STYLE GUIDANCE

Now you get to have all the fun. Here's the catch: You've got to know what looks good on you.

Figure out your body type and go from there. Once you know how to shop for your shape, you can begin to really rock your own individual style.

- We've got you covered if you're slender, top heavy, pear-shaped or curvaceous. Find the most flattering cuts for adorable tops, girlie dresses and skirts and perfect slacks and jeans.

- Now go exploring in your closet (or your mother's closet if she doesn't mind). Or just keep the tips in mind when you can afford your next shopping spree. And try before you buy.

- You've got the dress code for your job interview. And you've got your prom checklist. Now all you have to do is commit the fashion dos and don'ts to memory.

THE RIGHT CLUTCH

On your stroll, keep this fashionable clutch handy and within reach. If you're in a casual mood or if you need to go high-glam, you can take *The Diva-Girl's Guide to Style and Self-Respect* with you almost anywhere. It's more than a book, it's a relationship guide when it comes to dealing with your girlfriends and boyfriends. It's also a survival manual to keep you safe in the streets and on the information superhighway.

Take Your Stroll

Every girl has dreamed of profiling down a red carpet. Your Style Star get-up is sure to make the best-dressed list. And your face has Cover Girl all over it. You're turning heads, with your fly hairstyle, for all the right reasons.

Your wildest dreams are within your reach. It can be a Pulitzer Prize or Tony Award. You never know. Your red carpet in life could also be walking across the stage for graduation. Your red carpet could be you getting that competitive internship at a Fortune 500 company.

Or look at it like this: Your red carpet moment is every time you step out of your front door. You're presenting yourself to the world. People are checking what you do and how you do it. So while you're getting your package together, make sure you ooze some confidence. And DivaGirl, you won't have to worry about any trip-ups.

JUST LIKE YOU

* WYOMING, 17

Q: "I get nervous when I have to go to a fancy event. I always think I'm going to make a fool of myself. How do you work a room with confidence?"

Lisa Silhanek, Owner of Silhanek LLC
Helps Corporations Reach Women Through Fashion

A: "Approach and smile. Head up, hand out, heart open. Say, 'I'm Wyoming.' If your new friend does not reply with his/her name, ask.

If I were meeting you for the first time, I would ask how you came to be named Wyoming. This would give you a chance to put me at ease with a fun story or a wish that you had a simple name like Lisa. Then I would tell you how common my name is and that I am often called Lisa Number 2. We would laugh and then be great friends. I would find it easy to introduce you as I've learned your name.

I always say something nice next. 'I heard you say you were going to Spain. I love your tie. You smell great.' This allows the person to tell me something about him/herself. If they don't take the bait and start talking, I'll ask a question about the event—usually, where are the hors d'oeuvres?

PAY ATTENTION. People will tell you exactly what they want from you within the first few minutes of meeting them. So yes, try to use their name—it will help you to remember it—and more importantly, LISTEN. Really watch. The man whose tie you complimented will tell you his wife gave it to him and she's making the presentation tonight. Everyone wants you to know how they are connected to the event—so ask, nicely, and listen to the answer.

If I'm really stuck and conversation is not flowing, I'll ask why my new friend is here tonight. 'What brings you here tonight?' Be careful with the tone—you don't want to sound like your mom when she knows you are not where you are supposed to be!

I find that if I say hello with warm eyes directed at my new friend, I won't have to run away. If I'm getting nothing back, then I excuse myself and move on. I simply say, 'Excuse me.'

If I feel obligated, I might add a reason: 'I see a friend' or, 'I need another napkin.' Of course, if the person is shy but interested—he might go with you to meet your friend or get you a napkin.

If you are going to a business event and working the room—use the same warm gaze as you would for

your favorite relative, warm and interested with strength and dignity.

Facebook and Google have changed the way we interact but you will need the full name and contact information of your new friends to stay in touch. So carry your card (make one if you don't have a business-supplied card) and give it with a smile. Of course, if you choose not to share your information with someone, then take their card and don't over promise. What goes around comes around.

Good luck, Wyoming. I'm looking forward to meeting you!"

YOUR SPACE

Have you learned more new stuff about yourself? Here's your chance to fill in the blanks:

_____

What do you see yourself doing this time next year?

_____

_____

What do you see yourself doing in five years?

_____

_____

What do you see yourself doing in 10 years?

_____

_____

I know you can be whatever you want to be. If someone tells you otherwise, tune them out. Sing your own song, in your own key. And groove to your own beat. Whatever you decide to do with your life, do me one favor: Keep it fabulous, DivaGirl!

Polish until you sparkle. Sparkle until you shine!

Smooches!

Ms. Cheryl

Resource Guide

CHAPTER 7: DINING OUT
Answer Key:
1. C
2. C
3. C

The Advocate: Lesbian teens can find news and relevant information in this publication ~
www.advocate.com

Ambermag.com: Check out this beauty source for Black and Latina hair, beauty and style ~ **www.ambermag.com**

Amplify Your Voice: This is the online home of Youth Action Network of Advocates ~ **www.amplify yourvoice.org**

Art In Motion: is a movement created by Ford model/artist/philanthropist Monica Watkins. The movement seeks out and nurtures young, disadvantaged artists to grow, thrive, and effect positive change in the world through art and music ~ **www.artinmotionshow.com**

Black Aids Institute: This organization is geared toward addressing the AIDS epidemic in the Black community ~ **www.blackaids.org**

Black Girls Rock! You'll love this mentoring organization to promote the arts for young women of color ~ **www.blackgirlsrockinc.com**

Center for Young Women's Health: This site has helpful information for teen girls as they enter womanhood ~ **www.youngwomenshealth.org**

DermHA: Stop here to find skin-care products formulated for sensitive skin (free of fragrance, alcohol, dyes, and mineral oil) ~ **www.dermha.com**

Don't Let This Lipstick Fool You: This is the story of the making of WNBA champion Lisa Leslie

DoSomething.org: This is an organization that helps young people rock causes they care about ~ **www.dosomething.org**

Dove Campaign for Real Beauty: This is a movement that empowers girls with essential facts and information they need ~ **www.dove.us**

Dr. Susan's Girls-Only Weight Loss Guide: The easy, fun way to look and feel good! by Susan Bartell

EngineerGirl: This site encourages women and girls to consider engineering as a career ~ **www.engineergirl.org**

Fashion Institute of Technology: FIT sponsors summer classes for high school and middle school students to explore art and design, business and technology majors and develop art and design portfolios ~ **www.fitnyc.edu**

Everything You Ever Wanted to Know About
College: The title pretty much sums up this book
by Dr. Boyce Watkins

The Evoluer House: This is a non-profit organization
that empowers girls by nurturing positive self-
expression and personal development ~
www.evoluerhouse.org

**Girl's CEO Connection (Girl's Creating Enterprising
Organizations):** Its mission is to empower high
school girls (9th-12th grade) with entrepreneurial
and leadership skills; to empower them to create,
develop and market their businesses, while
positioning a "new" generation of women
entrepreneurs and leaders. ~
www.girlsceoconnection.wordpress.com

Girls Communicating Career Connections: The
site, aimed at middle-school girls, features a video
series created by girls, and companion educator
materials on science and engineering careers ~
www.gc3.edc.org

Girls Educational and Mentoring Services (GEMS):
This organization empowers girls and young
women, ages 12–24, who have experienced com-

mercial sexual exploitation and domestic trafficking to exit the commercial sex industry and develop to their full potential ~ **www.gems-girls.org**

Girls for a Change: It's GFC for short, a national organization that empowers girls to create social change ~ **www.girlsforachange.org**

Girls Inc.: This group inspires all girls to be strong, smart, and bold through a network of local organizations in the United States and Canada ~ **www.girlsinc.org**

Girlshealth.gov: This sites gives teens information about health, family life and other issues they may face ~ **www.girlshealth.gov**

Girl Scouts of the USA: It's the leadership development organization with girl and adult members worldwide ~ **www.girlscouts.org**

Girls Speak Out: It's a place where girls anywhere can find and express themselves ~ **www.girlsspeakout.org**

Healthy Menus for Teens: Disney Family offers its take on healthy kid-friendly menus and recipes ~ **www.family.go.com/food**

Helping Our Teen Girls in Real Life Situations: HOTGIRLS works to improve the health and lives of young Black women through programs inspired by hip-hop culture ~ **www.helpingourteengirls.org**

HIV Testing: You can get tested whenever you have a regular medical check-up. Or, to find a testing site near you, call **1-800-CDC-INFO (232-4636**) ~ **www.hivtest.org**

Hungry Girl: This amazing e-newsletter gives delicious healthy alternatives to our favorite fatty foods ~ **www.hungry-girl.com**

I-Safe: It stands for Internet Safety Education ~ **www.isafe.org**

I Wanna Know: This is a useful teen-centered website of the American Social Health Association ~ **www.iwannaknow.org**

J Lo: The Secret Behind Jennifer Lopez's Climb to The Top: Get an insider's look into J Lo's journey from Fly Girl to superstar by Sarah Gallick

Let's Move Campaign: The East Wing's challenge to help raise a generation of healthier kids is the brainchild of First Lady Michelle Obama ~ **www.letsmove.gov**

Life Is Not a Fairy Tale: This is a you-can't-keep-a-good-woman-down story by Fantasia Barrino

Logan Magazine: Young people with disabilities may find this publication of interest ~ **www.loganmagazine.com**

Love is Respect: Here, teens can gain insight on handling relationships ~ **www.loveisrespect.org**

MaDonna Grimes 3-in-1 DVD: This queen of hip-hop fitness dance brings you a 90-minute collection that helps you sculpt while you dance ~ **www.madonna-grimes.com**

Microsoft DigiGirlz Programs @ Microsoft: The company offers camps for high school girls to learn about careers in technology ~ **www.microsoft.com/digigirlz**

Miles to Go: The Disney star shares with her fans this coming-of-age story by Miley Cyrus

The Mint: It offers a website that gives teens tools for managing their money ~ **www.themint.org**

The Money Book for the Young, Fabulous & Broke: Your required reading list should include this financial-reality-check guide by Suze Orman

MyMoney.gov: It has money-management advice for teens, on saving, spending, and borrowing money, and more ~ **www.mymoney.gov/content/money-management-teens.html**

My Sistahs: This website offers information and support for women of color on sexual health issues ~ **www.amplifyyourvoice.org/mysistahs**

The National Dating Abuse Helpline: Call this helpline if you find yourself in trouble; **1-866-331-9474 or 1-866-331-8453 (TTY)**

National Domestic Violence Hotline: If you're being abused, contact **1-800-799-SAFE (7233)** or **1-800-787-3224 (TTY)**.

The National Eating Disorder Association: Visit here for treatment and prevention of eating disorders ~ **www.nationaleatingdisorders.org**

The National Sexual Assault Hotline: This confidential 24-7 hotline will connect you to your local crisis center **1-800-656-HOPE (4673)**

The National Youth Advocacy Coalition: NYAC is a social justice organization that advocates for and with young people who are lesbian, gay, bisexual, transgender, or questioning (LGBTQ) ~ **www.nyacyouth.org**

NetSmartz Workshop: This interactive site promotes Internet safety by the National Center for Missing & Exploited Children ~ **www.netsmartz.org**

New Moon: This online magazine is devoted to inspiring content for and by girl ~ **www.newmoon.com**

Our Story: Hear what these twin tycoons have to say in their official autobiography by Mary Kate Olsen and Ashley Olsen

Planned Parenthood: It is a trusted health care provider, an informed educator, a passionate advocate, and a global partner helping similar organizations around the world. Planned Parenthood delivers vital reproductive health care, sex education, and information to millions of women, men, and young people worldwide ~ **www.plannedparenthood.org**

Put on Your Crown: Life-Changing Moments on the Path to Queendom: The rapper-turned-Academy-Award-nominated-actress has quite a story by Queen Latifah

Quick and Dirty Secrets of College Success— A Professor Tells It All: Get through these challenging years with an insider's point of view by Dr. Boyce Watkins

Rosh Hodesh: It's a Girl Thing! Judaism is the basis of this educational program that enriches the lives of girls ~ **www.roshhodesh.org**

The Safe Schools Coalition is designed to improve the climate for LBGT students ~ **www.safe schoolscoalition.org**

Scarlet Teen: It offers sex education for teens in the real world ~ **www.scarleteen.com**

Serving From the Hip: 10 Rules for Living, Loving and Winning: Two of the best athletes in the world dish about success on and off the court by Venus Williams and Serena Williams

Sex, Etc.: This is a website that is written by teens, for teens, on teen sexual health issues ~ **www.sexetc.org**

Teen Latinitas: This magazine informs, entertains and inspires young Latinas to grow into healthy, confident, and successful adults ~ **www.latinitasmagazine.org/teens**

Teen Manners: From Malls to Meals to Messaging and Beyond: This guide takes a hip, teen-friendly look at etiquette by Cindy P. Senning and Peggy Post

Teen Wire: Visit Planned Parenthood's Teen Talk site ~ **www.teenwire.com**

USDA: This site encourages e-visitors to take control of their diet ~ **www.mypyramid.gov**

Women's Health: This agency provides informa-tion on shelters, counseling and legal aid ~ **www.womens health.gov**

Women's Sports Foundation: This group has information about scholarships, internships, training, fitness, careers, gender equity, homophobia, and disabilities ~ **www.womenssportsfoundation.org**

Wired Safety: Visit this website for information and resources for victims of cyber stalking, cyber bullying and cyber abuse ~ **www.wiredsafety.org**

Work It Out: This queen of hip-hop fitness tells curvy girls how to live a healthier lifestyle by MaDonna Grimes

WriteGirl: This is a nonprofit organization for high school girls centered on the craft of creative writing and empowerment through self-expression ~ **www.writegirl.org**

X-block: Designed for teens, this website not only promotes Internet safety, but also encourages teens to become mentors ~ **www.xblock.isafe.org**

YouthNoise: This site empowers teens to speak out about violence, child abuse, youth rights, HIV/AIDS and more to take action ~ **www.youthnoise.com**

Check out some of our DivaGirl's Guide experts:

Dr. Susan Bartell ~ www.4healthygirls.com

Millie Bell ~ www.dermha.com

Karen Bishop ~ www.karencbishop.com

Beverly Bond ~ www.blackgirlsrockinc.com

Warren K. Bradley ~ www.warrenkbradley.com

Eve ~ www.eve-360.com

MaDonna Grimes ~ www.madonna-grimes.com

DJ Diamond Kuts ~ www.djdiamondkuts.com

Kimmi Hendrix ~ www.kimmihendrix.net

Anthony Jones ~ www.evoluerconsultants.com

Monica ~ www.monica.com

Kenya Moore ~ www.kenyamoore.com

Eddie Pope ~ www.eddiepopefoundation.org

Rakia Reynolds ~ www.Philly360.com

Tiffany D. Sanders, Ph.D. ~ www.drtiffanysanders.com

Dr. Boyce Watkins ~ www.boycewatkins.com

Tina Wells ~ www.buzzmg.com

Sonja N. Williams ~ www.sonjanwilliams.com

Acknowledgments

From the beginning, there were two people who told me, "You don't have to be like everybody. Just be yourself." Hazel and Eugene Wadlington, my mommy and daddy. To you, I especially thank you for launching my career in the world of glamour. You instilled values in me that charted my course in life and allowed me to define success for myself. You never let me forget God is the rock upon which I stand. Early on, you taught me I had a responsibility to give back to help others along the way. Muahhh! I love you so much!

To all of my incredible family: my hubby David, Curtis, Jean, Linda, Chantay, Justin, Rahill, Rashida, Kenneth, Ramona, Brent, and my entire Wadlington, Woodards and Layton family, you are my foundation and ever-present source of strength. Thank you for loving and accepting me exactly as I am. I send you love from across the waters.

I want to single out for special praise Sheilah Vance, Esq., president of The Elevator Group, for believing in the book and mission and having patience with bringing my vision to life. I have been blessed with the remarkable skills and boundless support you brought to this project. Sonya Beard, thank you, SuperGirl, for your energy and encouragement in bringing that mission and vision to the page. What can I say? Your commitment and diligence … you are simply splendid!

Dr. Cornel West, thank you, sir, for being on board with this project from its infancy. Your endorsement put the icing on the cake. I will be forever grateful. An additional heartfelt thank you to Renee Cardwell Hughes and Dr. Jason King. I so appreciate your taking time out of your busy schedule to give your blessing of endorsements to this project.

To my famed N.Y.C. fashion and beauty power circle—Anthony Jones, Karen Bishop, Darya Latham, Raphael Monroe, Micah McDonald, Debra Ginyard, and William Robinson—you bring the joy, life, laughter, and creative juice to my existence. You'll never know the depths of my appreciation. Merci!

Tina Byers, thank you: You're a dynamo. You're generous with your passion, support, and Rolodex. You got the ball rolling, finding dynamic women for the book. Darlise Blount-Harrison, my gifted GirlFriend—you've been with me for decades on the front line, advocating for girls—thank you for stepping up to find more women who rock. Thanks to Sheila Simmons for defining what a Diva Girl is. Thank you Stefani Vance-Patience for your artistic eye and magic fingers. Warren K. Bradley thanks for your illustrations in the hair gallery and in *She's Got To Have Fit*.

The book would not have been possible without all the magnificent publicists, managers, and agents: Patricia Coates, Esq., Karen Taylor-Bass, Theola Borden at RCA Music Group/J, Arista, RCA Records, Barry Florence, Skai Blue Media, Anton Moore, Elena Ellie Cox, Kevin Harry, Karen Pope, Shauntay Hampton.

Mere words can't express my gratefulness to you for prioritizing my requests.

My friends and associates lent a hand wherever necessary. I'm blessed to have the hand-holding and pats on the back from friends who supported this book from Page 1. Girls around the world will all be better because of the good deeds of the following people: Gerda Gallop-Goodman, Anita Lewis, Elmer Beard, Cindy Bass, Lisa Silhanek, Bobbi Booker, Willard A. Stanback, Esq., Sherry Howard, Loraine Ballard Morrill, Patty Jackson, Fatimah Ali, Nancy Gilliam, Dame Jennifer Smith, Carlton Tyrell, Sarah Dash, Loris Diran, Ethel S. Barnett, The Evoluer House Board of Directors, Julie Wilch, Rhonda Walker, Jasmine Sudler, Ciara Robinson, Ashley Fuller, Jeannie Wright, Sylvia Scott, Imani Pendergrass, Carletta Williams, Corey Stewart, Nyderiah Smith, Fatimah Underwood, Tyleah Davis, Craig Williams, Ross Schwartz, Monica Watkins, Roy Campbell, Kristin Haskins-Simms, The Hon. Paula A. Cox, JP, MP, Yolanda Arnold, Mellanie Lassiter, Shamara, Desirae Holland, Shawn Rhea at Planned Parenthood. To the Philadelphia and the National Association of

Black Journalists, a major thanks. You jumpstarted my journalistic journey. Karen Quinones Miller, thanks Mama—you told me that no one could write this book but me. Tamara Jeffries, big props Lady, for writing my winning book proposal.

I am honored to be in the company of such a distinguished list of amazing people who were willing to share their words of wisdom with girls everywhere. Thank you Monica, Eve, Kenya Moore, Beverly Bond, Lisa Silhanek, DJ Diamond Kuts, Dr. Boyce Watkins, Dr. Joycelyn Elders, Tiffany Sanders, Ph.D., Tina Wells, Sonja Williams, Anthony Jones, Karen Bishop, William Robinson, Kimmi Hendrix, Dr. Susan Bartell, the late Mia Amber Davis, Debra Ginyard, Micah McDonald, Millie Bell, Darya Latham, Police Chief Jeri Williams, Eddie Pope, Judith Peters, MaDonna Grimes, Rakia Reynolds, Amiya Alexander, Bridgeja' Baker, Amber Liggett, for offering your voices to make a difference in the lives of our precious young pearls. I am extremely grateful to you.

DIVAGIRL'S GUIDE REMEMBERS
SELF-IMAGE ICON THE LATE MIA AMBER DAVIS

Blowing kisses to heaven, I am eternally grateful to our shining star the late Mia Amber Davis, a role model for people of all colors, shapes and sizes, an angel who got her wings, but left a legacy of greatness and goodness. Mia sprinkled incomparable jewels on the pages of *The DivaGirl's Guide to Style and Self-Respect*. Her life, victorious success and contributions to this book will inspire girls everywhere. She lives in the hearts of many—and thus, will never die or be forgotten.

About the Authors

Cheryl Ann Wadlington is one of the nation's premiere fashion and beauty journalists and a leading consultant in the field of personal growth. An accomplished writer, television personality and sought-after motivational speaker, she has reached millions through publications such as *Self*, *Essence*, *Life & Style*, and *The Philadelphia Daily News*. She founded Evoluer Image Consultants, an award-winning full-service agency in Philadelphia that provides clients with extensive makeovers, personal shopping and wardrobe management. She also operates the nonprofit organization, The Evoluer House, which has graduated more than 700 socio-economically challenged girls from this highly successful personal development program. Cheryl majored in advertising and communications at the Fashion Institute of Technology and Fashion Merchandising at Bauder Fashion College. She also served on the faculty of the Temple University School of Communications and the advisory board of Cheyney University's Fashion Merchandising program.

Sonya Beard, a nationally award-winning newspaper reporter, spent more than five years at *In Style*, the international fashion magazine at Time Inc. She served as a media consultant for Kulture2Couture, a fashion initiative by the Mayor's Office of London. She's also a freelance book editor for fashion and beauty titles, including *Soul Style: Black Women Redefining the Color of Fashion* and *Black Hair: Art, Style and Culture*. The Temple University grad is based in Seoul, where she's been a contributing writer for *Seoul* magazine and an expat correspondent for *The Korea Herald*.